The Log House in East Tennessee

The
LOG HOUSE
in East Tennessee

JOHN MORGAN

The University of Tennessee Press ■ Knoxville

Copyright © 1990 by The University of Tennessee Press / Knoxville.
All Rights Reserved.
Manufactured in the United States of America.
First Edition.

The paper in this book meets the minimum requirements of the American National Standard for Permanence of Paper for Printed Library Materials. ∞ The binding materials have been chosen for strength and durability.

Library of Congress Cataloging in Publication Data

Morgan, John, 1944–
    The log house in East Tennessee / John Morgan. — 1st ed.
       p.   cm.
    Includes bibliographical references.
    ISBN 0–87049–652–2 (cloth : alk. paper)
    ISBN 0–87049–653–0 (pbk. : alk. paper)
    1. Log cabins—Tennessee   I. Title.
NA8470.M67   1990
728′.37′09768—dc20   90–11912   CIP

Dedicated to
Professor Leonard W. Brinkman

Contents

CHAPTER ONE
Introduction 1

CHAPTER TWO
Antecedents, Diffusion, and Dominance
of Midland Log Construction 7

CHAPTER THREE
Log House Construction in East Tennessee 19

CHAPTER FOUR
The Historical Pattern of House Construction
in Blount County 43

CHAPTER FIVE
Persistence of Log House Construction 59

CHAPTER SIX
Socioeconomic Factors and the Decline
of Log House Construction 79

CHAPTER SEVEN
Sawmilling and Lumbering and the Decline
of Log House Building 87

CHAPTER EIGHT
Innovations in Construction Techniques and the Decline
in Log House Building 98

CHAPTER NINE
Conclusion 108

Notes 117

Bibliography 135

Index 159

Illustrations

Maps

1. Blount County, Tennessee 5

2. Distribution of Log Construction in the Eastern United States 9

3. The Counties of East Tennessee 21

4. Distribution of Blount County Pre–Civil War Houses 48

5. Distribution of Blount County Houses Constructed During the 1860s 50

6. Distribution of Blount County Houses Constructed During the 1870s 52

7. Distribution of Blount County Houses Constructed During the 1880s 55

8. Distribution of Blount County Log Houses Constructed During the 1890s 57

Figures

1. Notch Types Common in the Eastern United States 12

2. Typical Log Single-Pen Unit 22

3. Typical One-and-a-Half-Story Single-Pen Log House 22

4. Sided One-Story Single-Pen Log House 23

5. Two-Story Single-Pen Log House 24

6. Hewn Log Wall 25
7. Stone Chimney in Gable End of Single-Pen Log House 26
8. "Stick-and-Mud" and Stone Chimney 27
9. Grainger County Log House with Original Board Roof 28
10. Central Chimney or Saddlebag Double-Pen Log House 31
11. Cumberland Double-Pen Log House 32
12. Dogtrot Double-Pen Log House 32
13. Half-Dovetail Notches on Log Pen 37
14. V Notches on Thompson-Brown House 38
15. Saddle Notches on Round Logs 39
16. Square Notches on Collapsed Log Wall 40
17. Blount County House Construction, by Type and Period of Construction 44
18. Thompson-Brown House 46
19. Warner Martin House 46
20. Maclin Kerr House 47
21. Single-Pen Log House of 1870s 54
22. Frame "I" House of 1880s 54
23. Elijah Oliver Log House 66
24. Timber Frame Construction 67
25. Balloon Frame Construction 100
26. Board-and-Batten Box House 103

Tables

1. Single-Pen House Forms in Three East Tennessee Counties 29

Illustrations ■ xi

2. Notch Types in Grainger, Morgan, and Blount Counties, as Related to Type of Wood   35

3. Number and Distribution of Carpenters in Blount County, 1870   71

4. Value of Real Estate and Personal Property for Frame and Brick House Dwellers in Blount County in 1860   77

5. Value of Real Estate and Personal Property for Log House Dwellers in Blounty County in 1860   78

6. Characteristics of Blount County Frame House Builders During the 1870s   82

7. Characteristics of Blount County Log House Builders During the 1870s   83

Acknowledgments

My interest in the cultural landscape and log construction began when I was a graduate student at East Carolina University and was inspired by a dynamic teacher-scholar, Charles F. Gritzner, a student of Fred Kniffen, pioneer of American folk architecture studies. Encouraged by the example of Gritzner's work on log housing in New Mexico, I sought to understand better the changing status of folk structures in the traditional tobacco landscape in my native region of eastern North Carolina. In addition to Gritzner, Professors Donald Steila, Douglas Wilms, and the late R.T. Jollie made important contributions to my early professional development, for which I am grateful.

As a graduate student at the University of Tennessee, I was introduced to the cultural landscape of Appalachia and the Upland South by another Kniffen student, Professor John B. Rehder, who also gave me the opportunity to participate in historic buildings surveys in several East Tennessee counties. Field data for this study were obtained primarily from those surveys, which were conducted for the Tennessee Historical Commission and the Blount County Historic Trust. I am grateful to those organizations for use of survey data; to Steve Rogers of the Tennessee Historical Commission for his support of this project; and to the following dedicated survey participants who were always willing to hike an extra mile to an abandoned house or spend an extra hour chasing down an elusive source: Vincent Ambrosia, Allen Arbogast, Eddie Bright, Neal Cyganiak, Jennifer Dehart, Stan Guffey, Beth Lohman, Ashby Lynch, Walter Martin, Michael Mayfield, Joy Medford, Andy Williams, David Williams, Jon Williamson, Bethany Worley, and David Wray. I also would like to acknowledge the contributions of hundreds of East Tennessee's rural folk, especially homeowners, who allowed examination of their structures and provided essential information about them. Additional field investigations and library research for this project were supported by grants from McNeese State University and Emory and Henry College.

My gratitude is extended to Michael DeVivo, Gary Freedom, Sidney Jumper, Frank Leuthold, Adele McKenzie, Joy Medford, and Lisa Roberts for comments and suggestions that improved this work; to Terry Jordan, Edwin H. Hammond, and Tyrel Moore for encouragement and advice; to Thomas Fox and David Wray for photographic assistance; and to Beth Wood and Lynn McKinney for drawing the illustrations. My greatest debt is owed to my dissertation director, Professor Leonard W. Brinkman, whose criticisms made this research a challenge and whose encouragement made the challenge an exciting experience. Finally, I wish to thank my wife, Sally, son, Jack, and daughter, Jessie, whose support, patience, and sacrifices helped make completion of this work possible.

Parts of this book were previously published in the *Proceedings of the Conference on Appalachian Geography* and in the *Tennessee Anthropologist*.

CHAPTER ONE

Introduction

The log house is an important element in the settlement heritage of much of the eastern United States. Numerous students of the cultural landscape have described the tradition of horizontal log construction in works ranging from detailed small-area studies to general studies of log housing in large areas.[1] In some areas log construction was seldom practiced, and in others the log house was an important landscape feature only during the pioneer period. In yet other areas, particularly the Upland South, of which East Tennessee is an integral part, the log house dominated the landscape for a much longer period. In such areas, log construction typically was not replaced by frame construction until the latter half of the nineteenth century, and in some locâles the log house remained the dominant dwelling until the early part of the twentieth century.[2] The vast amount of literature on the log house has been devoted mainly to understanding its origin and diffusion and the geographic variations in its form and construction characteristics. Surprisingly, research dedicated to understanding the processes responsible for the decline of log house construction is lacking.

This book examines the cultural history of the East Tennessee log house, the predominant farm structure for at least the first one hundred years of the region's history. Although log construction played a significant role in the historical development of East Tennessee and thousands of log structures remain on the landscape today, little research on the log house has been undertaken previously.[3] This work will comment on antecedents of the East Tennessee log house, describe its characteristics, and account for the decline in its construction. The search for the origin of the East Tennessee log house has been undertaken in existing published works, the characteristics of the structure have been derived from the data of historic buildings surveys in eight counties, and the analysis of construction history has been achieved through an indepth single-county case study.

The value of studying an area's traditional housing has been emphasized by several cultural geographers, including John Fraser Hart, who stated that "perhaps nothing tells so much about the values a man holds as the kind of house in which he chooses to live." In making that selection, the dweller "is able to demonstrate his artistry, advertise his beliefs, and flaunt his wealth."[4] According to Fred Kniffen, a pioneer in the study of traditional American architecture, housing "reflects cultural heritage, current fashion, functional needs and the positive and negative aspects of non-cultural environment."[5] Examination of major changes in an area's housing character is important because such a change often is indicative of significant modifications in the basic economy or culture.[6] As Peirce Lewis has stated, "If a people changes its collective mind about its houses, there is a good chance it has changed its mind about many other things as well."[7]

The primary intent of this work is to account for the decline in log house construction in East Tennessee. Although no research has been devoted specifically to the study of the decline of log house construction, several scholars have mentioned factors responsible for its decline in various areas of the eastern United States. Terry G. Jordan attributed the decline in log dwelling construction in Texas, at least in part, to a social stigma associated with living in the log house, and Eugene M. Wilson has stated that in Alabama the change from log to frame housing was a step "toward higher social and economic status."[8]

Carl Lounsbury associated the decline of log house construction in North Carolina to the passing of frontier conditions and the rise of a market-oriented agricultural economy.[9] Richard Pillsbury related the persistence and decline in log house construction in Pennsylvania to the "local economic situation," with log construction persisting longer in "areas of least economic development."[10] Regional economic status was one of the factors associated with the decline of log house construction in Ohio, according to historian Donald A. Hutslar, who wrote that, by the middle of the nineteenth century, "the log house had become confined to the rapidly disappearing, unsettled areas and to the less economically successful sections of the state."[11] Stanley Willis attributed the decline of log construction in southwestern Virginia to regional economic change. He noted that the persistence of the log house "often corresponded to the remoteness of the area," with residents in Dickenson County, for example, living "in log houses until the railroad, timber, and coal industries appeared shortly after World War I."[12]

Other writers have attributed the decline in log house construction to the changing status of sawmills and greater availability of lumber in rural areas. Historian Ronald D. Eller indicated that the log structure was the dominant dwelling type in remote areas of rural Appalachia before the 1880s and 1890s, because "the long distances to sawmills made the construction of frame structures impractical outside of the village and valley communities."[13] The construction of frame houses thus was "made increasingly feasible by the construction of neighborhood sawmills."[14] Geographer Wilbur Zelinsky surmised that the log house was ubiquitous during the frontier era in Georgia but steadily declined in number prior to the Civil War as well-to-do families began to construct frame and brick houses. He attributed the log house's post-Civil War demise to the proliferation of sawmills, which made frame construction possible even for the poor classes.[15]

Innovations in frame construction may have played a role in the decline of log house construction. Before the mid-1800s, most of the frame houses built in the United States were constructed with heavy or timber framing, but since that time the majority of frame houses have been built with light or balloon frames.[16] Hutslar has observed that log houses no longer were being constructed in most of Ohio by the mid-nineteenth century, and that "the balloon frame house had become the standard reasonably priced housing."[17] Wilson reported that the balloon frame house replaced the log dwelling in Alabama between 1875 and 1920.[18]

Statements in the literature about the causes of the decline of log house construction generally have alluded to large areas, and such statements have not been supported by detailed empirical evidence. The various reasons given for the decline of log construction therefore are, in effect, mere assertions, and none should be accepted until tested empirically in a specific area. It was the author's belief that an initial effort to identify and understand processes responsible for the decline of log construction was best undertaken through a small-area case study. Identification of processes associated with the decline of log house construction either would confirm or contradict the various sequences proposed in the literature. Naturally, although findings from a single case study could be expected to contribute to overcoming the inadequacies of the literature, the study would have to be replicated in other areas before findings could generally be accepted.

Blount County was chosen as the area in which to examine the decline of log house construction because it contains a large number of extant nineteenth-century houses, including more than two hundred log dwellings, and because construction histories are available for a large number of the houses (map 1). Although the landscape of Blount County has changed substantially during the past several decades, log houses remain scattered throughout the inhabited portion of the county. The widespread distribution of log houses allows a researcher to describe accurately the past local variations in house construction types. Most of the mountainous southeastern part of the county lies within the Great Smoky Mountains National Park, created in 1930.[19] The great

Introduction ■ 5

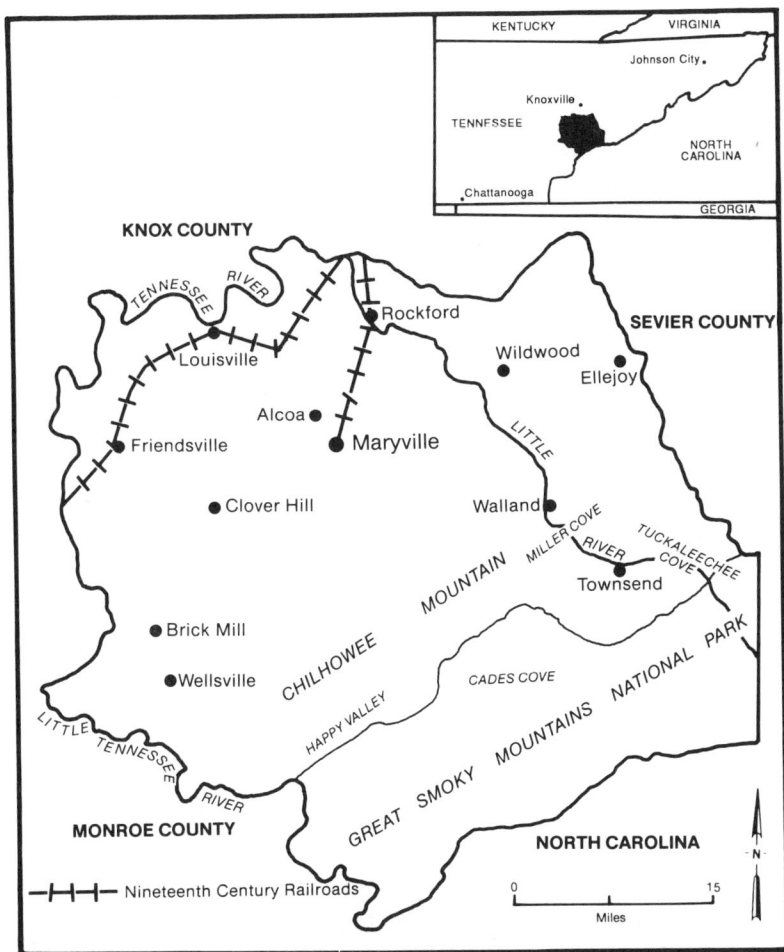

Map 1. Blount County, Tennessee.

majority of the area now in the park was uninhabited before the park was established. A few log houses may have been destroyed as the park was established, but not enough to alter greatly the distributional pattern. In Cades Cove, where several hundred persons resided during the nineteenth century, the National Park

Service preserved a number of log structures, but most frame houses in the cove were destroyed.[20]

Basic characteristics of Blount County's structures were recorded during a historic buildings survey conducted for the Tennessee Historical Commission and the Blount County Historic Trust from 1982 to 1984.[21] The buildings survey was part of the State of Tennessee's long-range program to inventory each county's historic and architectural resources. Survey procedures required that all passable roads in the county be travelled in an effort to locate every structure more than fifty years old. Building locations were plotted on 7.5 minute topographic maps, basic form and construction characteristics were recorded, and efforts were made to determine the construction dates of the houses. Dates for many of the houses were obtained through interviews with county residents, especially descendants of original house owners. Construction histories of a few houses were discovered in local newspaper articles, and construction dates for many of the houses were estimated based on characteristics of the structure and/or partial construction histories furnished by local residents. Socioeconomic data on original owners were gathered primarily from government documents, especially population and agricultural census records.

Information on the social and economic history of Blount County was taken from both primary and secondary sources. The most important primary sources were the U.S. censuses for Blount County, including the unpublished schedules for both population and agriculture. County court records, nineteenth-century newspapers, and elderly informants were also of considerable value. Regional and local histories were the most valuable secondary sources, and Inez E. Burns' *History of Blount County,* A. Randolph Shields' *The Cades Cove Story,* and Durwood Dunn's *Cades Cove* were especially useful research aids.[22] Books, journals, magazines, newspapers, and nineteenth-century travel journals provided background information on the social and economic history of East Tennessee and the United States.

CHAPTER TWO

Antecedents, Diffusion, and Dominance of Midland Log Construction

Log buildings were not common in all the early American colonies. English settlers, who formed the largest ethnic group of colonists, were not familiar with log construction in the British Isles and initially did not build log structures in the New World.¹ They erected the frame and half-timber structures that were characteristic of their native land.² Early houses of Dutch settlers were "bark huts, pit homes, and frame cottages" but not log dwellings. As soon as they could, many Dutch settlers built brick houses styled after those common in their European homeland.³

Log construction was introduced to eastern America in 1638 by Finns and Swedes who settled in the New Sweden Colony in the Delaware Valley.⁴ The Swede-Finn tradition of horizontal log construction was firmly established among several ethnic groups by the time Germans brought a knowledge of log construction to southeastern Pennsylvania during the early 1700s.⁵ Although most log construction and form characteristics were likely Finnish or Scandinavian in origin, other Delaware Valley ethnic groups, including English, Scotch-Irish, and Germans, made significant contributions to the area's architecture. The result was a syncretic log architecture created by America's first "melting pot."⁶

From this Middle Atlantic hearth or core, particularly southeastern Pennsylvania, waves of nonslaveholding yeomen farmers migrated westward and southward, carrying with them the tradition of log construction. The domain of the Middle Atlantic hearth or core is referred to as the Midland culture area.[7] An extension of the Midland culture area is the Upland South culture area, where log construction remained a characteristic culture trait during much of the nineteenth century (map 2). The concept of the Upland South culture area was first put forth by historian Frederick Jackson Turner, who considered it "an extension of the old Middle Region, chiefly from Pennsylvania." Turner delimited the area as being "between the falls of the rivers of the South Atlantic colonies on the one side and the Allegheny mountains on the other."[8]

The limits of the Upland South vary considerably on existing maps of American culture areas. Jordan and Rowntree and Zelinsky use similar delimitations of the Upland South, including most of the states of West Virginia and Kentucky; the western halves of Virginia and North Carolina; upper South Carolina and Georgia; northeastern Alabama; Tennessee, with the exception of the extreme western section; extreme southern Ohio, Indiana, and Illinois; and the Ozark areas of Missouri, Arkansas, and Oklahoma. In addition, Jordan and Rowntree include southern Oklahoma and central Texas on their map of the Upland South.[9] The map of Milton Newton, however, portrays the Upland South as considerably larger in area. Of particular significance is Newton's extension of the Upland South eastward in the Carolinas and southward to include almost all of Georgia, Alabama, and Mississippi.[10]

Field studies in Europe by Jordan and Kaups have revealed the great impact Finnish and Swedish settlers had on Midland and Upland South log architecture. Northern European contributions to log carpentry included V, square, full-dovetail, half, diamond, and saddle notchings; chink construction; the use of both round logs and logs hewn on two sides; and the ridgepole-and-purlin roof with board covering. Architectural forms whose origins can

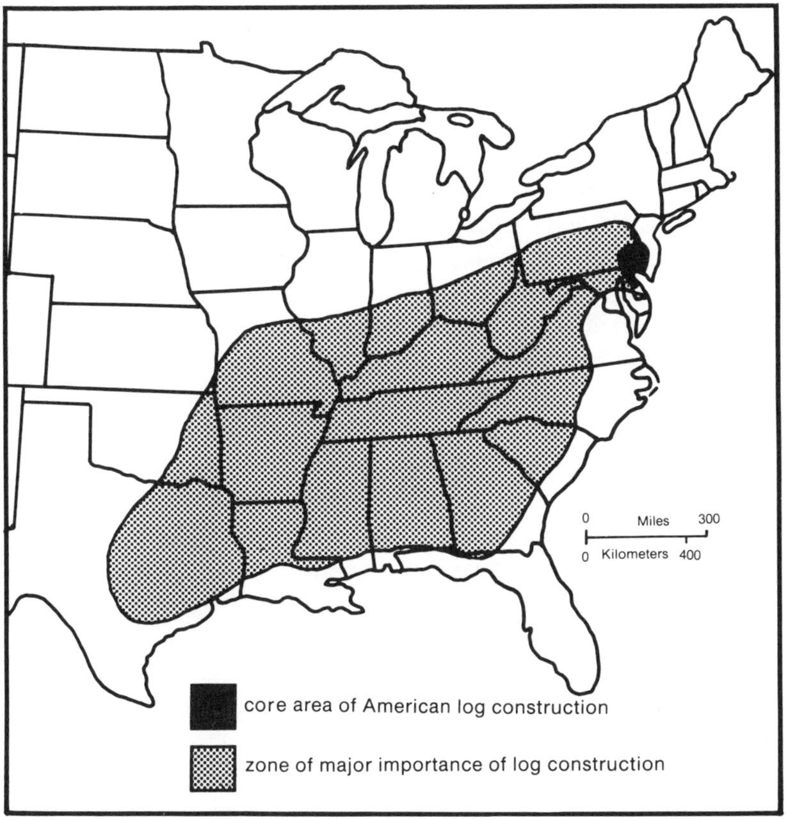

Midland Log Construction ■ 9

Map 2. Distribution of log construction in the eastern United States. Source: Modified from Jordan, *Texas Log Buildings*, 26, and Jordan, *American Log Buildings*, 8.

be traced to Finland and Sweden are the dogtrot house, the single-pen cabin with gable-end door, the single-crib barn, and the double-crib barn.[11]

German contributions to the tradition of log architecture were also significant, and include the shingled roof, the Pennsylvania barn, the continental central-chimney log house, board gables, tall thin planking, and the rafter roof. In addition, the Germans modified and refined Fenno-Scandian V notching and reinforced the use of the dovetail notch, chinking, and the double-crib plan.[12] British settlers influenced Midland architecture by contributing two forms of the single-pen cabin, two types of double-pen dwellings, and the centrally placed gable-end chimney.[13]

Jordan contends that understanding Zelinsky's "doctrine of first effective settlement" is important in explaining the role of Finns and Swedes in the development of American log construction. The doctrine holds that "the specific characteristics of the first group able to effect a viable, self-perpetuating society are of crucial significance for the later social and cultural geography of the area, no matter how tiny the initial band of settlers may have been." Because Finns and Swedes carried out the first effective settlement of the lower Delaware Valley, the log buildings constructed by them served as models for subsequent pioneer settlement in the Midland area.[14]

Log construction was carried in several directions by emigrants from the Midland core area, but it did not effectively penetrate New England or the Tidewater South.[15] In addition to its presence in Pennsylvania, southwestern New Jersey, and central and western Maryland, Midland log construction diffused over great distances westward and southward. The westward movement penetrated the southern parts of Ohio, Indiana, and Illinois and southern and central Missouri. The southern and southwestern movements carried log construction through West Virginia and Kentucky; western and piedmont Virginia, North Carolina, and South Carolina; most of Georgia, Alabama, and Mississippi; all of Tennessee and Arkansas; eastern Oklahoma; and central and eastern Texas (map 2). Although the directions of the main flows of log construction were to the west, southwest, and south, a multitude of routes off the main flows proceeded in all directions.[16]

By the time the log house had spread relatively short distances from Pennsylvania, its form had become nearly uniform. The single-pen (one structural unit with four log walls joined together by corner notches) log house with exterior gable-end chimney became the syncretic dwelling and was transported great distances to the west and south. Sometimes the house was enlarged by erecting a second log pen beside the first unit to form a double-pen structure. The diffusion of log construction from southeastern Pennsylvania was not limited to log houses. Ideas about other buildings, particularly barns and outbuildings, were carried across the frontier as part of the cultural heritage of settling groups. Small rectangular outbuildings with cantilevered front gables became common throughout the Upland South, but log barn types varied considerably from area to area.[17]

The most distinctive feature of horizontal log construction is the corner notch, a device which locks the logs in place. Because notch types tend to exhibit considerable spatial variation across the eastern United States, their distribution has been used to show patterns of the diffusion of log construction. Kniffen stated that different types of notches "were favored by different groups of American pioneers and there were changes with time and with the distance that they were carried from the point of introduction." By plotting notch types on maps, one can discern the geographic pattern of diffusion.[18]

Three notch types, the V, saddle, and full-dovetail notches, were common in southeastern Pennsylvania (fig. 1). The V was the dominant notch type in the area and was used especially to erect houses and more substantial barns and outbuildings. The full-dovetail notch was employed to a lesser extent but for the same purposes as the V notch. The saddle notch was used primarily to construct lower-quality barns and outbuildings. All three notches were carried by the Germans and Scotch-Irish into central Maryland and the northern Shenandoah Valley in the 1730s. The V notch, however, became the dominant type carried from the Shenandoah Valley eastward into the Blue Ridge Mountains and southward into the Valley of Virginia. The V notch continued to dominate further south and west through the Valley of Southwest Virginia and East Tennessee, across Tennessee and eventually into Arkansas and Texas.[19]

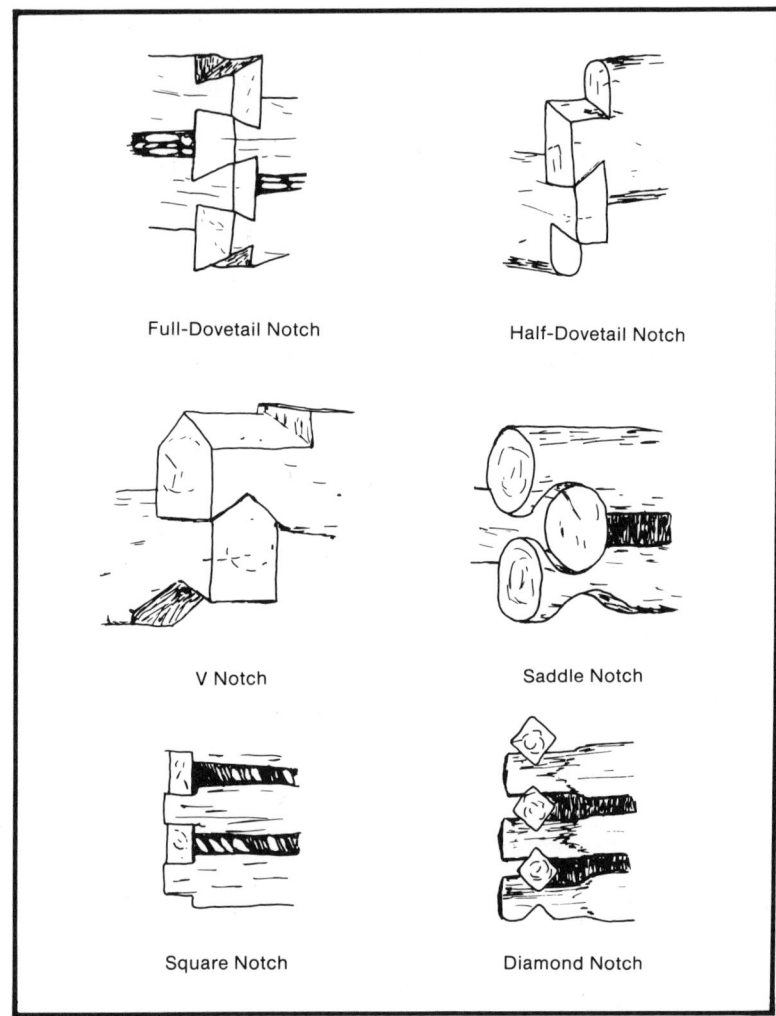

Fig. 1. Notch types common in the Eastern United States. Source: After Kniffen and Glassie, "Building in Wood," 53, 55.

East of the Blue Ridge in Virginia, settlers adopted Midland log construction, but developed or employed a variety of notch types, including square, saddle, half-dovetail, and, to a lesser degree, half, diamond, and full-dovetail notches (fig. 1). The half-dovetail notch dominates in western North Carolina, whence it was carried westward into Tennessee.[20]

All three common Midland notches—V, saddle, and full-dovetail—spread from Pennsylvania down the western Appalachian valleys, and all are found in the Alleghenies along the northern section of the West Virginia–Virginia border. In this area, however, the half-dovetail notch is commonly used, and it becomes dominant farther south in West Virginia, eastern Kentucky, and southwestern Virginia. Many barns and outbuildings in those areas are saddle notched.[21] The two Appalachian flows, one moving through the Valley of Virginia and the other through the Alleghenies, merged in the area of southwestern Virginia, northwestern North Carolina, and upper East Tennessee. In this area, saddle, V, and half-dovetail notches all commonly appear, though saddle notches are found mainly on barns and outbuildings.[22] Patterns of corner notches in East Tennessee thus result largely from the southward diffusion of V, saddle, and half-dovetail notches from Virginia and the westward diffusion of half-dovetail and square notches from North Carolina.

The forested Upland South was settled rapidly by migrants from the Midland core. Backwoods frontiersmen, especially Scotch-Irish but also including Germans, Welsh, English, Swedes, and Finns, began leaving the core region about 1725 and had reached as far as East Tennessee by 1750.[23] John Solomon Otto and Nain Estelle Anderson attributed the rapid conquest of the vast hardwood and pine forests of the Upland South to the settlers' utilization of a woodsland-adapted agricultural economy, in which forest lands were substituted for scarce labor and capital. Forest lands were devoted to open-range herding and a fallow-oriented system of extensive farming.[24]

Jordan and Kaups contend that the ability of Midland settlers to conquer rapidly a vast wilderness was derived from the Finns, who "were preadapted for life in the American backwoods" and "enhanced their fitness by accepting from the Delaware Indians certain other adaptive elements." The preadaptive traits included individualism, a scattered settlement pattern, shifting cultivation, open-range livestock farming, and log carpentry skills. The survival skills of the Finns and Indians were shared with other groups through ethnic mixing and intermarriage.[25] Milton Newton, who also claimed that preadaptive traits gave settlers the ability to conquer the frontier quickly, stated that such traits were learned in a backcountry hearth extending from Lancaster, Pennsylvania, to Augusta, Georgia.[26]

Log construction was the accepted practice in the Upland South during the frontier period, and in many parts of the area it was common during most of the nineteenth century. Travelers reported the presence of log buildings over broad areas during the late eighteenth and early nineteenth centuries. Gilbert Imlay described house construction on the Kentucky frontier during the 1790s:

> As the country gained strength, the stations began to break up in that part of the country, and their inhabitants to spread themselves, and settle upon their respective estates. But the embarrassment they were in for most of the conveniences of life, did not admit of their building any other houses but of logs . . . A house of this sort may be made as comfortable and elegant as any other kind of building; and is therefore the most convenient, as it may be erected in such a manner as to answer the circumstances of all descriptions of persons.[27]

The Frenchman F.A. Michaux traveled extensively in the eastern United States during 1802 and reported the presence of large numbers of log houses in Pennsylvania, Ohio, Kentucky, Tennessee, the Carolinas, and Georgia. In commenting on the upper Carolinas, Michaux stated that the inhabitants of the upper Carolinas lived much as those of Tennessee and Kentucky did. "They reside . . . in loghouses isolated in the woods, which are left open in the night as well as the day."[28]

Frame and brick houses were erected quite early in towns on the frontier, but log dwellings constituted a significant portion of all houses in smaller nucleated settlements, especially during their early development. Michaux described Knoxville, Tennessee, in 1802 as comprising about two hundred houses, "chiefly built of wood," but nearby Kingston was described as consisting of thirty or forty log houses.[29] In Greeneville, Tennessee, he observed about forty houses, "constructed with square beams something like the log houses," but saw only houses built of wood in Jonesboro.[30] Michaux observed that Paris, Kentucky, a "manor-house for the county of Bourbon," contained more than a hundred and fifty houses, "half of which are brick."[31] He noted that brick houses made up most of those in Lexington, described as the wealthiest town in the three new western states. In contrast, Gallipolis, Ohio, located along the Ohio River, was reported to consist "solely of about sixty loghouses," and nearby Alexandria, Ohio, had about twenty houses, mostly log structures.[32]

Although the proportion of log dwellings in towns decreased through time, they did not disappear quickly from the landscape or lose their identity through modification. In Middle Tennessee towns, for example, log dwellings were observed during the 1830s. Eastin Morris described Gallatin as a town with "thirty-five log, thirty-eight frame, and twenty-seven brick houses, on the first day of June 1830." According to architectural historian James Patrick, Nashville still had twenty-one log houses in 1831.[33] Relatively few log structures, however, are believed to have been constructed in towns of the South after the 1830s.

Log buildings continued to be erected in the rural South for several decades after the demise of log construction in towns and villages. Frederick Law Olmsted provided evidence that the log house was still a very common feature in several parts of the South during the 1850s.[34] In his travels he observed "poor whites" in central Mississippi and the northern Alabama hill country living in log houses. His description of the dwellings of noncotton farmers of the hill country shows the dominance of the log house over the frame house:

> The larger number of the dwellings are rude log huts, of only one room, and that unwholesomely crowded. I saw in and about one of them, not more than fifteen feet square, five grown persons, and as many children. Occasionally, however, the monotony of these huts is agreeably varied by neat, white, frame houses . . . I passed the night at the second framed house that I saw during the day.[35]

Olmsted found the nonslaveholding cotton farmers of northern Alabama living in similar structures: "The country continues hilly, and is well populated by farmers, living in log huts, while every mile or two on the more level and fertile land, there is a larger farm, with ten or twenty negroes at work."[36] The area along the border of southeastern Tennessee and northeastern Alabama also was dominated by log dwellings, with "two detached cabins usually forming the habitation of a family."[37] Olmsted also referred to the presence of log dwellings in East Tennessee, western North Carolina, and southwestern Virginia.

In summer 1865, John Richard Dennett traveled to the South to report on its post–Civil War conditions for *The Nation*, a magazine published in New York.[38] His observations revealed the presence of many log houses in the Piedmont of southern Virginia and the Carolinas. His description of houses around Danville, Virginia, revealed the dominance of the log house in that area but also indicated the presence of two other classes of houses: "At rare intervals one sees the mansion-house with pretensions to elegance and comfort, the log-cabin plastered with mud occurs very frequently, and somewhat less often is seen the ordinary farm-house."[39] In the "sandy pine country" of North Carolina, along the Cape Fear River, about fifty miles north of Fayetteville, Dennett found the houses to be "seldom more than a log hut."

He had a similar description of the houses in the poor, sparsely-settled Congaree River area of South Carolina.[40]

Dennett did not always find log houses to be mere "huts" of the poor. Occasionally he encountered the "better" class living in log dwellings. One example was near Marion, South Carolina:

> This man owned a farm of more than two hundred acres . . . lived in a very neat log-house, with a trim yard around it, his outhouses and fences were regularly disposed and in good order, nine or ten books were on the mantlepiece, and his surroundings generally, as well as his manners and conversation, showed him to be a good deal above that class commonly called "low-down, triflin' people," or poor white trash.[41]

The writings of Scotsman Robert Somers indicate that the log house was still the dominant dwelling type among cotton planters in the Tennessee River Valley of Alabama in 1870–71.[42] His description of the typical houses and farmsteads of that area portrays the log house more favorably than did some earlier writers:

> Save in the vicinity of towns, where the planters sometimes build houses and ride out to their plantations, or some famous old homesteads in the country where the wealth of a former generation has erected mansions and offices more in style of the rural gentry than of the farmers of England, the planters for the most part live in plain log-houses, with a wide open hall running through the middle of it from a verandah in the front to a dining apartment and kitchen in the rear. . . . The dwelling-houses, besides having more or less well-chosen sites, are usually surrounded by a spacious courtyard, snake-fenced on its four sides, with stable for saddle and buggy horses, smoke-house, cotton-shed, corn-cribs, and uncovered pens for feeding milch cows . . . ranged round the exterior of the yard. . . . Cabins for the negro domestic servants and other right-hand persons about the planter are also put up near the homestead, so that . . .the log-house becomes the centre of a considerable establishment.[43]

After traveling to Nashville and northward to Louisville, Somers commented that regional variations in housing were discernible at that time in the Upland South. He found the houses on farms north of Nashville and in Kentucky to be more substantial than those of the cotton plantations.[44]

It is clear that the log house was common in the Upland South after the Civil War, but areal variations in the types of construction and the historical patterns of persistence and decline of log construction within areas are not well understood. It is known, however, that log houses did persist and were still being built in the early twentieth century in some of the more isolated areas of the southern mountains. For example, there were only 2 or 3 frame houses among the 42 houses in the Hazel Creek Valley of mountainous western North Carolina in 1904, and in the Bent Creek area of Buncombe County, North Carolina, 90 of 104 houses constructed before 1900 were made of logs.[45] The writings of John C. Campbell indicate that log houses were common in the Southern Highlands during the early 1900s, and Mandel Sherman and Thomas R. Henry found "hollow folk" of the Blue Ridge Mountains living in log dwellings in the late 1920s.[46]

CHAPTER THREE

Log House Construction in East Tennessee

Log construction in East Tennessee paralleled the pattern in the Upland South as a whole. In addition to houses, barns, and farm outbuildings, many other buildings, such as forts, courthouses, jails, hotels, taverns, stores, churches, schools, grist mills, and blacksmith shops were built of logs during the frontier era. Decades after the end of the frontier period, large numbers of log structures, especially houses, barns, smokehouses, and corn cribs, continued to be erected and were the dominant types in some areas.[1]

After the Civil War, the log house remained an important landscape feature in East Tennessee. In fact, J.B. Killebrew characterized the houses of East Tennessee as generally being of log construction in the 1870s, and specifically named Knox and Bledsoe as counties with log house dominance.[2] As with the larger Upland South region, it is difficult to be specific about the decline of log house construction in East Tennessee. In some areas log construction may have declined soon after the Civil War, but in other areas log house construction persisted into the present century.

An agricultural and industrial survey conducted by the Tennessee Valley Authority in 1934 showed nearly 14 percent of the houses in Grainger County to be of log construction, and a farm housing survey revealed that nearly 12 percent of Sevier County's houses were log in 1939.[3] There is reason to believe that the percentage of log houses in East Tennessee in the 1930s was even higher than reported in the surveys. It is likely that some isolated and/or abandoned log houses were omitted or not sampled, and it is probable that some sided log dwellings mistakenly were reported as frame structures.

Historic building surveys of eight East Tennessee counties, undertaken in the late 1970s and early 1980s by the Tennessee Historical Commission, revealed that large numbers of log buildings, especially houses, remain part of the landscape.[4] More than eight hundred log houses were identified in Blount, Grainger, Union, Morgan, Hamblen, Jefferson, Meigs, and Unicoi counties, and more than seven hundred log structures (houses and other buildings) were identified in Blount and Grainger counties alone (map 3). Although, at the time of writing, the number of log structures was dwindling rapidly, evidence still existed allowing for the documentation of a rich tradition of log construction in the East Tennessee area.

Types of Log Houses

Examination of data from surveys in Blount, Grainger, and Morgan counties suggested that 85 percent of surviving log dwellings in East Tennessee were single pen-structures, which Henry Glassie described as "the typical house of all settlers from Maryland to Alabama."[5] A single pen consists of one structural unit of four log walls (fig. 2). The single-pen house characteristically had side-facing gables, an exterior gable-end chimney, and a roof ridge parallel to the front of the structure (fig. 3). The single-pen interior might consist of one room or be divided by a partition wall into two rooms.

Approximately 65 percent of the single-pen houses examined in the three counties (Blount, Grainger, and Morgan) were one-and-a-half-story structures, whereas about 25 percent were one-story and about 10 percent were two-story structures (figs. 3–5). The log dwellings typically were built one to two feet above

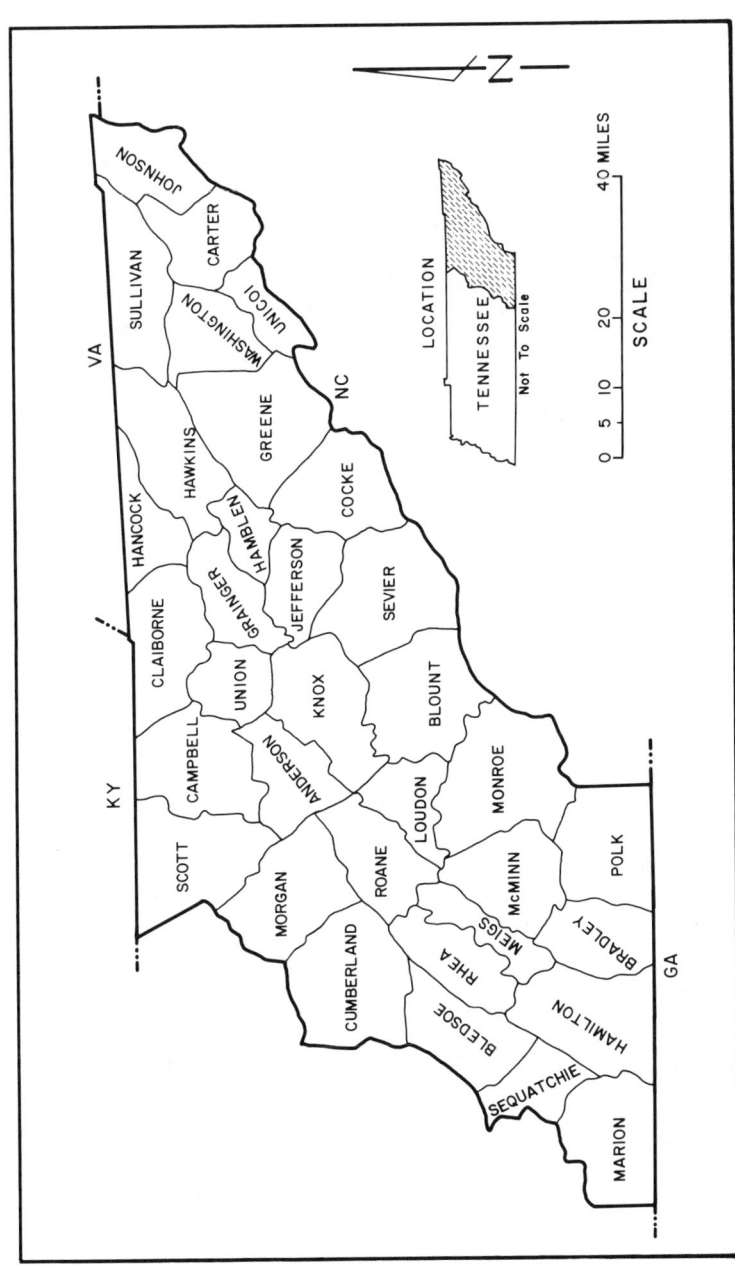

Map 3. The counties of East Tennessee.

Fig. 2. Typical log single-pen unit (Grainger County, 1978).

Fig. 3. Typical one-and-a-half-story single-pen log house, with side-facing gables and central gable-end chimney (Grainger County, 1979).

Fig. 4. Sided one-story single-pen log house (Morgan County, 1980).

ground on stone piers or on a solid stone foundation, and had wooden floors, although during the pioneer period some structures had earthen floors. Chink wall construction, in which logs of the front and rear walls are placed in layers alternating with logs of side walls to leave spaces between the logs, was used to erect virtually all East Tennessee log houses studied. The chinks or spaces between the logs were usually filled with small pieces of wood and daubed with mud or mortar (fig. 6). Logs typically were ten to twenty inches in diameter and hewn, on sides only, to a width of approximately six inches.

A chimney was constructed in the center of a gable end on nearly all the single-pen log structures. Chimneys typically were of stone or brick, but a few "stick-and-mud" chimneys have been

24 ■ The Log House in East Tennessee

Fig. 5. Two-story single-pen log house, built in Grainger County around 1830. Collapse of chimney revealed the house to have log extending to the apex of the structure in the gable end, which indicates that the house has a ridgepole-and-purlin roof (1981).

recorded (figs. 7 and 8). The structures commonly had front and rear doors, usually placed in or near the center of the walls. No windowless houses were observed, but several had only one window, in either the front or the gable end of the building. Most houses had two or more windows, although some had been added since the original construction. One-and-a-half-story houses often had loft windows in the gable and occasionally had small upper windows in the front of the house. Two-story houses usually had both front and side second-floor windows, but sometimes the end opposite the chimney had no window.

Front porches had been added to a majority of the East Tennessee log houses, and some of the structures had rear porches. Nearly all the log houses surveyed had metal roofs, but the original

Fig. 6. Hewn log wall showing pine logs with chinks or spaces between logs filled with small pieces of wood and daubed with mortar (Blount County, 1983).

roofs usually had been covered with wooden boards, although occasionally tapered shingles were used (fig. 9). In the great majority of cases, roofs were supported by rafters, and on some of the log houses, the roof was extended two to four feet on the chimney side to protect the chimney from the elements.

Most of the single-pen log houses had been sided, and at least 85 percent had been enlarged with frame additions. Nearly half the houses had end or side frame additions, many of which were gable-roofed extensions of the main structure. Approximately 75 percent of the extant log dwellings had rear additions, of which about half were gable-roofed ell additions and half were shed additions. The rear additions usually contained the household kitchen. During earlier periods many structures had detached kitchens, which were either self-contained units or connected to the main house only by an open porch. Few such kitchen units

Fig. 7. Stone Chimney in gable end of single-pen log house, built of poplar logs in Grainger County, c. 1840 (1980).

remain today, but at least six still existed in Blount County at the time of writing (fig. 23).

Henry Glassie identified two basic types of single-pen houses in the southern mountain region of the United States: the rectangular pen and the square pen. Jordan subsequently discovered the same pen types in Texas. The rectangular single-pen log house

Fig. 8. Stick-and-mud and stone chimney, built on Davis house in Blount County a few years after the Civil War (1984).

Fig. 9. Grainger county log house with original board roof. The structure was erected around 1930 (1980).

was introduced in this country by the Swedes or Scotch-Irish of the Middle Atlantic colonies, whereas the square house is an English product, a descendant of the sixteen-foot-square British one-bay house.[6]

Log structures with the front and rear walls at least five feet longer than the side walls are classed as rectangular. Glassie found that the rectangular pens of the southern mountains were twenty feet or more in length. Those with front and rear dimensions less than five feet longer than the side dimensions are classified as square; that pen is normally about sixteen feet square, and the dimensions are almost always within two or three feet of being equal.[7]

Of log pens measured, 39 percent of those in Morgan County, 31 percent of those in Grainger County, and 30 percent of those in Blount County could be considered rectangular, based on the classification of Glassie and Jordan (table 1). Rectangular structures in the three counties ranged in size from 18x13 feet to 36x18 feet. Commonly observed pen dimensions were roughly 26x20, 25x20, 26x18, 24x18, 25x17, 24x16, 22x16, and 20x15 feet.

Table 1

Single-Pen House Forms in Three East Tennessee Counties

County	Number of Structures	Percent Rectangular	Percent Square	Percent of Square Houses at Least 20 Feet Wide	Percent of Square Houses with Front Greater Than Two but Less Than Five Feet Longer Than the Side
Grainger	54	31	69	81	89
Morgan	31	39	61	63	84
Blount	123	30	70	70	63

Source: Compiled by the author from Historic Buildings Surveys in the three counties and from measurements of structures.

Sixty-nine percent of Grainger County single-pen dwellings, 61 percent of Morgan County structures, and 70 percent of those in Blount County had front and rear walls less than 5 feet longer than side walls (table 1). The dimensions of the structures ranged from 16 feet square to 24x22 feet. Unlike the square pens observed by Glassie in the southern mountains and by Jordan in Texas, few of those in Grainger, Morgan, or Blount counties were 16 feet square. In fact, only 37 percent of pens in Morgan, 19 percent in Grainger, and 30 percent in Blount were less than 20 feet in length. Most of the square houses in the three counties had front and rear dimensions which, in contrast to the findings of Glassie and Jordan, were more than 2 and less than 5 feet longer than the side dimensions (table 1). Frequently occurring square pens were approximately 22x18, 20x18, 21x18, 20x17, 24x20, 22x20, 18x16, and 20x16 feet.

Dimensions for many single-pen log houses in Grainger, Morgan, and Blount counties did not fit precisely into the rectangular- and square-pen classification of Glassie and Jordan but instead represented a range of dimensions between those of the rectangular and square pen categories. Such findings may constitute evidence of a fusion of types of log architecture in the Upland South.

One of the advantages of the pen tradition of log construction was the ease with which a house could be enlarged by the addition of a second pen. A significant number of double-pen houses were built in the nineteenth century in East Tennessee, and fifty-one were identified during the surveys conducted in Grainger, Blount, Morgan, and Union counties in the late 1970s and early 1980s. Single-pen houses in the Upland South typically were enlarged by one of three methods.[8] The addition of a second pen to the chimney end of a single-pen structure resulted in a central-chimney "saddlebag" house, believed to have been a British invention (fig. 10).[9] Twenty-three saddlebag log houses were identified in the four counties.

A second method of enlargement consisted of building a pen that abutted the gable end opposite the chimney of the original

Fig. 10. Central chimney or saddlebag double-pen log house in Union County. The larger, taller right pen was built a few years before the left pen (1980).

pen. Such a structure is referred to as a "Cumberland" house, and twelve such houses were located (fig. 11). The Cumberland house, which takes its name from the Middle Tennessee region where many such houses have been identified, is another British creation.[10]

The third method of enlargement also consisted of construction of a second pen adjacent to the gable-end opposite the chimney of the original pen. In this method, however, an open passageway or "trot" was left between the two pens. This type of double-pen dwelling is referred to as a "dogtrot" house, and it diffused to this country from eastern Finland.[11] Sixteen log dogtrot houses were identified in the Grainger, Blount, Morgan, and Union county surveys (fig. 12).

Double-pen houses usually were built in stages, but sometimes both pens were constructed simultaneously. If a house was built in stages, the two pens usually differed in one or more characteristics, the most obvious being notch type, wood type, log size and

Fig. 11. Cumberland double-pen log house, characterized by side-by-side pens, a front door in each pen, and a gable-end chimney (Grainger County, 1980).

Fig. 12. Dogtrot double-pen log house with stone chimneys on gable ends (Jackson County, Ala., 1978).

shape, and pen dimensions. Pens built simultaneously would have the same notch type and often the same dimensions. In Blount County, several were connected by one central wall, an indication that the pens were erected at the same time. Nearly one-third of the Blount County double pens were built simultaneously and not in stages. Of the ten double pens erected, five were saddlebags, four were Cumberland houses, and three were dogtrots. Each of the saddlebag and Cumberland houses was built with one central wall shared by two pens.

Various writers have referred to the log dogtrot house as a type dominant throughout Tennessee. Edna Scofield, for example, stated in 1938 that "the so-called 'double-pen' log house with the open hallway between the two pens is the basis of a large percentage of all house types in Tennessee."[12] Recently, James A. Crutchfield, writing about pioneer architecture in Tennessee, asserted, "The dogtrot cabin gained acceptance rapidly, and its popularity spread throughout Tennessee and the rest of the region."[13] Although the dogtrot house is common in some parts of Tennessee, especially the southeastern and central parts of the state, it certainly was not the dominant house type in nineteenth-century East Tennessee.[14] Moreover, on the basis of the surveys in Blount, Grainger, Morgan, and Union counties, it seems clear that the saddlebag and not the dogtrot is the most common type of double-pen house surviving in East Tennessee. It was reported in 1987 that the saddlebag also was the dominant double-pen log dwelling in a section of nearby western North Carolina.[15]

The number of stories that comprised East Tennessee log houses appears to have varied temporally. The one-and-a-half-story unit dominated from the days of earliest settlement until the late 1800s. The proportion of one-story log houses constructed in the area increased through time, so that nearly all the log structures erected during the twentieth century have been of one story. Two-story log dwellings commonly were constructed in East Tennessee before 1860, but few have been built since that time.

There was an apparent relationship between the affluence of

an owner and the number of stories in a log house. During the period in which the log house was the dominant dwelling type, most farmers lived in one-and-a-half-story structures, two-story log houses generally were built by more affluent residents, and one-story log structures were occupied by relatively poor people. Two-story log double-pen houses are designated by scholars as "I" houses, and such houses are taken as symbolic of economic attainment in the Upland South.[16] The I house, first identified by Fred Kniffen in Indiana, Illinois, and Iowa, is a two-story structure, two rooms wide and one room deep. The I house was linked to larger, more prosperous nineteenth-century farms in a study of six East Tennessee counties.[17] After the Civil War, few two-story log houses were built, in part because affluent farmers constructed frame houses. By the time the one-story house became the most common log dwelling in the late 1800s, its construction was undertaken primarily by poor people.

Timber and Notch Types

Numerous tree species yield timber acceptable for use in log house construction, but in East Tennessee the great majority of builders seem to have used pine, poplar, or oak logs. In Grainger, Morgan, and Blount counties, pine apparently was the most commonly employed wood, accounting for 51 percent of the houses catalogued. Eighteen percent of the houses surveyed in the three counties were built with poplar, whereas 11 percent were constructed of oak. Nearly all the remaining 20 percent were constructed of more than one timber type, especially pine and oak or pine and poplar, depending upon the locale (table 2).

The extent to which pine was used varied significantly, with 66 percent of the houses examined in Blount County being of pine, 49 percent of those in Morgan, and only 36 percent of those in Grainger County. Poplar also varied greatly among the three counties. It was found on 28 percent of the Grainger County log houses and 22 percent of those in Morgan County, but it appeared

Table 2
Notch Types in Grainger, Morgan, and Blount Counties as Related to Type of Wood

		Pine	Poplar	Oak	Mixed
Number Observed		152	53	34	61
Type	%	%	%	%	%
Half-dovetail	66	64	77	53	67
V	22	17	19	44	26
Saddle	4	10	1	3	0
Square	4	7	4	0	3
Mixed	3	1	1	0	6

Source: Compiled by the author from Historic Buildings Surveys and from firsthand observation.

as a principal wood type in only 5 percent of the Blount County log dwellings. Distribution of oak log houses did not vary as greatly as that of pine and poplar structures. Grainger County had 13 percent of surveyed houses built of oak, whereas Blount had 11 and Morgan 9 percent. Mixed-timber construction showed little variation, occurring in between 18 and 23 percent of the log houses in each county.

The geographical variation of wood types in log houses appears to reflect variations in the historical distribution of certain timber species, especially pine and poplar. In Grainger County, for example, the great majority of log houses found north of Clinch Mountain were built of poplar logs, whereas those on the south side of the mountain were generally of pine construction. In Union County, bordering on northwestern Grainger County, poplar log houses also dominated. In Blount County, the few poplar log houses were found in or adjacent to the eastern mountainous areas of the county. Both pine and poplar must have been acceptable to the log house builder in all four of the counties. The variations in distribution of species, however, limited the choices available to house builders in some areas.

The connection of log walls to each other is made possible by the use of corner notches, which lock the logs securely in place. Several types of notches are common in the eastern United States, and four of them are found in East Tennessee.[18] Data on corner notches for eight counties surveyed in the 1970s and 1980s indicate that the half-dovetail notch was the dominant type found on East Tennessee log houses surveyed in the 1980s (fig. 13). In seven counties—Unicoi, Morgan, Meigs, Jefferson, Grainger, Union, and Blount—more than half the houses were erected with half-dovetail corners (map 3). The percentages of half-dovetail notches range from 58 percent in Blount County to a high of 88 percent in Unicoi County. Only in Hamblen County, where 58 percent of the houses were joined at the corners with V notches, the half-dovetail notch did not dominate (42 percent).

The V notch was the second most important notch type in East Tennessee. In addition to being the most common type in Hamblen County, where 58 percent of the houses were V-notched, the V notch also was common on houses in Grainger (27 percent), Blount (24 percent), Meigs (17 percent), and Union (12 percent) (fig. 14). Other notch types appearing on significant numbers of log houses surveyed were the saddle notch in Morgan County (22 percent) and the square notch in Blount County (10 percent) (figs. 15 and 16).

Several scholars have discussed factors responsible for selection of corner notch types. Kniffen believes that "cultural tradition" is the determining factor in the selection of notch type.[19] Jordan, although recognizing the influence of ethnicity on geographical patterns of notch types, asserts that in Texas notch type tended to vary with timber type: "In general, we can say that dovetailing predominated for hardwoods, while saddle, 'V', square, and semilunate notchings are prevalent in softwoods."[20] Folklorist Warren E. Roberts has stated that the distribution of hardwood and softwood forests is significant in explaining the pattern of corner notching in the eastern United States:

> V-notching and dovetail notching were closely associated with hewn logs, that is logs whose inner and outer faces are hewn

Log House Construction in East Tennessee ■ 37

Fig. 13. Half-dovetail notches on thin-planked log pen (Grainger County, 1979).

Fig. 14. V notches on Thompson-Brown house, Blount County (1984).

Log House Construction in East Tennessee ■ 39

Fig. 15. Saddle notches on round logs of Morgan County pen, built around 1930 (1981).

Fig. 16. Square notches on collapsed log wall of Blount County pen (1983).

away so that the wall, when it is built, is only six or seven inches thick. Hewing flourishes in areas where hardwood logs are used. Saddle notching, on the other hand, is used mainly with logs that are left in the round, and round logs are found mainly where softwood logs are used. Hence a map of the distribution of corner notching is not of much use unless it takes into account the question of where hardwood and softwood forests predominate.[21]

In assessing the relationship between timber patterns and notch types, Newton and Pulliam-DiNapoli, however, found that in Louisiana, "Notch types did not even change according to timber."[22]

Examination of data on timber and notch types for three counties (Blount, Grainger, and Morgan) reveals no evidence that timber type was the most important factor in selection of notch type in East Tennessee. The proportion of notch types associated with individual wood types generally paralleled the ratio of individual notch types to the total number of houses with notched logs. For example, half-dovetail, the notch type most common in the three counties, was the one most popular for each wood type, including pine, a softwood (table 2). An unexpected pattern, however, was found on oak log houses examined in Grainger County. Twice as many oak log structures were V-notched as were half-dovetailed, but in all there were only sixteen structures with oak logs. Conversely, 64 percent of Blount County's oak buildings were dovetailed, as were all four of those in Morgan County. It is clear that Jordan's hypothesis that hardwoods are dovetailed and softwoods are V-notched has not been confirmed in East Tennessee.

The data also tend to refute the statement by Roberts. A large number of East Tennessee log houses were erected with pine logs, but the saddle notch was rarely used, except on structures of relatively recent construction. Also, only on recently built log houses were logs left "in the round." The overwhelming majority of surviving nineteenth-century log houses of softwood construction were built of hewn logs—contrary to Roberts' contention.

The general pattern of corner notches observed in East Tennessee appeared to correspond with the areal variations identified by Kniffen and Glassie. The counties nearest the Valley of Southwest Virginia had higher proportions of V notches than those farther south or along the North Carolina border. The half-dovetail notch, which was common throughout the area, probably diffused to East Tennessee from western North Carolina and southwestern Virginia. The V notch apparently spread down the Valley of East Tennessee from Virginia. The square notch probably spread westward to Blount County from North Carolina, because it is common east of the Blue Ridge and because a study by Morgan and Medford of log houses in Grainger County, in upper East Tennessee, revealed only one square-notched house among 146 structures for which notch types were determined. The saddle-notched houses of Morgan County were built during the present century, and their construction was not associated with a particular culture group, but rather represented a simplification of log construction methods common in the twentieth-century South. It is apparent that tradition and not wood type was the factor most important in the selection of corner notch types by East Tennessee log house builders.[23]

To this point, the East Tennessee log house has been placed in a cultural context and the characteristics of the building's form and construction have been described. The next five chapters will examine the pattern of persistence and decline in log house construction in East Tennessee through an in-depth study of the case of Blount County.

CHAPTER FOUR

The Historical Pattern of House Construction in Blount County

A nalysis of the causes of the sharp decline in log house construction in Blount County cannot be carried out without knowing when and where log, frame, brick, and stone house construction occurred in the county during the nineteenth century. The historical and geographical pattern of house construction that is described below emerged primarily from analysis of data collected during a survey of all types of historic buildings, conducted in Blount County from 1982 to 1984. Of the more than 4,000 buildings surveyed, 927 houses were built before 1905. Construction histories, characteristics, and locations of these 927 buildings provide data for a reconstruction of the history and geography of the remaining nineteenth-century houses of Blount County. The data were supplemented by historical information, including interviews with elderly residents of the county and accounts by contemporary observers, printed in nineteenth-century newspapers.

Pre-1860 Period

The survey documented the presence of 127 houses known to have been erected before 1860. Seventy-two (57 percent) of these struc-

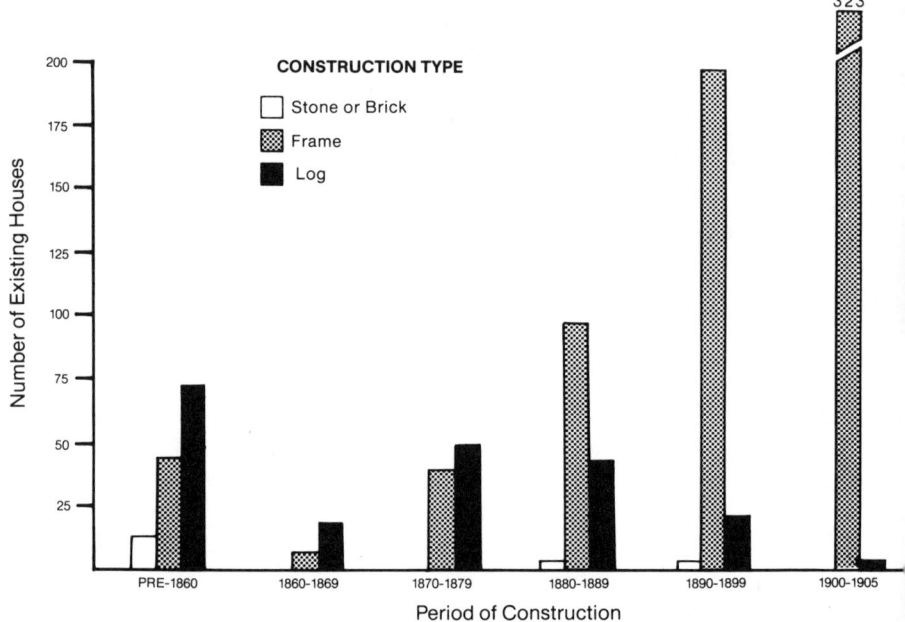

Fig. 17. Blount County house construction, by type and period of construction.

tures were log, whereas 43 (34 percent) were frame, ten (8 percent) were brick, and two were stone (fig. 17). There is little doubt, however, that a greater proportion of pre-1860 brick and stone houses remained on the landscape in the early 1980s than of pre-1860 log houses. The vagaries of time, particularly fires and lack of upkeep, are more destructive to log houses than to the more-substantially built brick and stone houses. Probably more pre-1860 frame houses have survived than log houses, but it is known that some frame houses in Blount County towns, especially Maryville, were burned during the Civil War.[1]

Permanent white settlement of Blount County began about 1786, when migrants arrived from North Carolina and Virginia.[2] Although few of the frontier houses remain today, there is reason to believe that a greater majority of the early houses were log structures. Most of these frontier houses were single-pen log structures with one-and-a-half stories, although some one- and two-story single-pen houses, as well as some double-pen structures, were erected. Numerous examples of pre-1860 log houses in Blount County, a few of them dating back to the first years of permanent settlement before 1800, existed at the time of writing (fig. 18).

In addition to the early log houses, surviving houses include several of brick, stone, and frame construction dated to the early 1800s, and at least one stone and one frame house erected in the 1790s (fig. 19). Several of the early frame houses were one-story two-room structures with a central chimney. Later, such two-room structures often became rear ells of larger houses. The brick and stone houses tended to be two-story I houses, characterized by having two rooms on the second or upper floor situated over two rooms on the lower floor (fig. 20).[3] The number of houses not made of logs that were constructed in the county increased during the 1840s and especially the 1850s, when numerous two-story frame "I" houses were built. The log house, however, continued to be the dominant construction type throughout the pre-Civil War period.

Maps showing the locations of pre-1860 houses remaining in Blount County in the early 1980s reveal different distributional patterns for log and nonlog houses (map 4). Log houses appear scattered through nonmountainous parts of the county, but houses made of brick, stone, and frame show a more concentrated pattern. Pre-1860 nonlog houses are found primarily (1) in the broad valley section which extends through Blount County from northeast to southwest, (2) along the Tennessee and Little rivers, and (3) in Louisville, an early port on the Tennessee River (map 1).

The locations of brick, stone, and frame structures evidently were more dispersed in the 1850s than in previous periods, but were still concentrated in the northern part of the county, especially along the Little River and in the valley section near Rockford and Wildwood (map 1). The more rugged, isolated eastern

Fig. 18. Thompson-Brown house, a double-pen structure with enclosed dogtrot, built in Blount County in 1790s. In the 1980s the house served as the Blount County Tourist Information Center (1983).

Fig. 19. Warner Martin house, built c. 1794, is the oldest existing frame house in Blount County. Warner Martin sawed lumber at his nearby water-powered sash sawmill to construct the house (1984).

Fig. 20. Maclin Kerr house, built in Blount County in 1847. The structure is an example of an "I" house, a two-story dwelling with the main unit being two rooms wide and one room deep. The "I" house was associated with agricultural opulence in the Upland South.

and southern parts of the county contain no known existing frame, brick, or stone houses built before 1840. Maps of existing houses, however, at best are general indicators of the past, and probably there were a few nonlog houses in areas which did not contain any at the time of the survey.

The county seat of Maryville had numerous frame houses before the Civil War, but they were either destroyed during the war, obliterated by urban expansion, or simply lost to the processes of old age. In other towns or villages in the county, especially Friendsville, Louisville, and Rockford, several pre-1860 houses are known to have been destroyed.

Before 1860, then, the log house was the dominant construction type in Blount County and its distribution corresponded to the general pattern of settlement. Nonlog houses, however, were constructed by a minority of families before the Civil War, and

48 ■ The Log House in East Tennessee

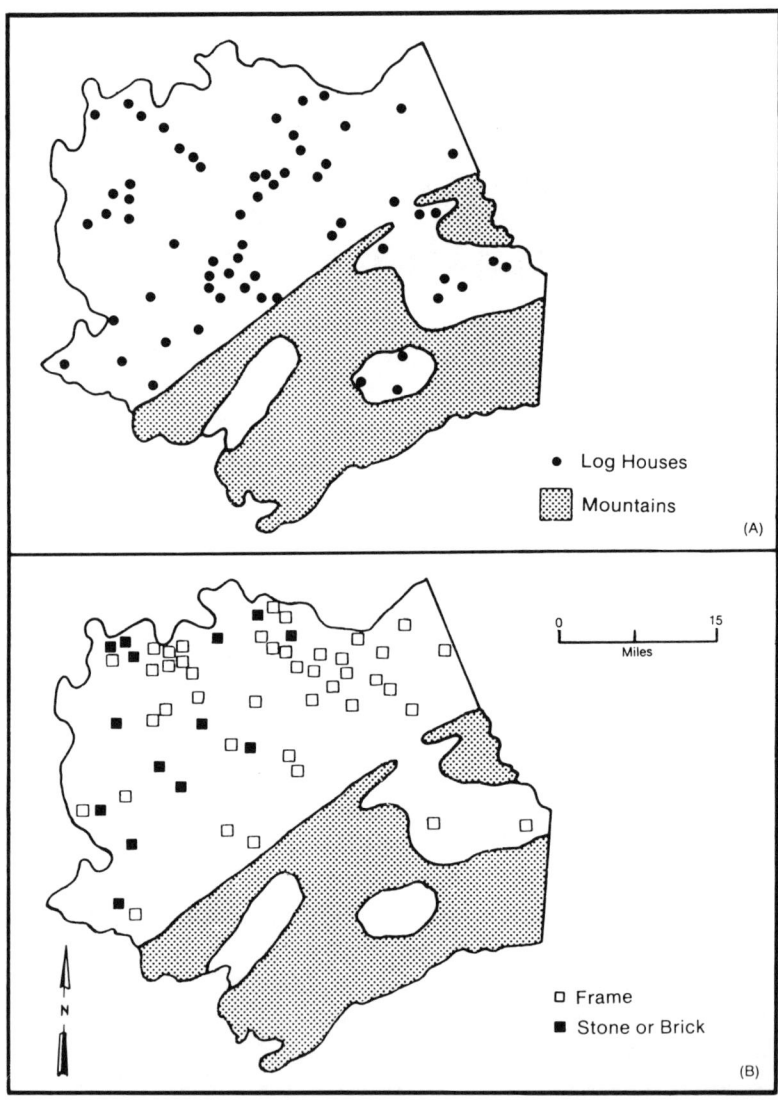

Map 4. Distribution of Blount County pre–Civil War houses existing in 1984.

such dwellings were located primarily in the northern part of the county. The locations of surviving nonlog houses are mainly in towns or villages, especially Louisville, and in the better agricultural lands—along the rivers and in the broadest valley in the county. It is also worthy of note that the concentration of nonlog houses in the northern part of the county may reflect, to some extent, the influence of the area's proximity to Knoxville, the urban center of mid–East Tennessee at that time.

Post-1860 Period

The Civil War greatly disrupted the social and economic life of East Tennessee. Damage was inflicted by both Federal and Confederate troops, house building declined greatly, and in some sections of the county, it came to a virtual halt.[4] The war so disrupted Blount County life that some houses under construction at the beginning of the war were not completed until the end of the war. Virtually all the houses completed during the war were log structures. House building increased after the Civil War, but during the late 1860s there continued to be considerably more log than frame construction. No brick or stone houses survive from the 1860s (fig. 17).

The locations of surviving houses built during the decade reveal a sparse but distinctive pattern (map 5). In the northern area of the county, where numerous houses, including some frame structures, were erected in the 1850s, house building appears to have been virtually nonexistent. Most of the extant houses were built in a belt parallel to and slightly west of Chilhowee Mountain (map 1). It is likely that this rugged area was affected less by Civil War activity than the less-isolated northern part of the county, which included the towns of Maryville and Louisville and the village of Rockford.

The decade of the 1870s was the last in which more log than frame houses seem to have been erected in the rural areas of Blount County. In some communities of the county, however, as

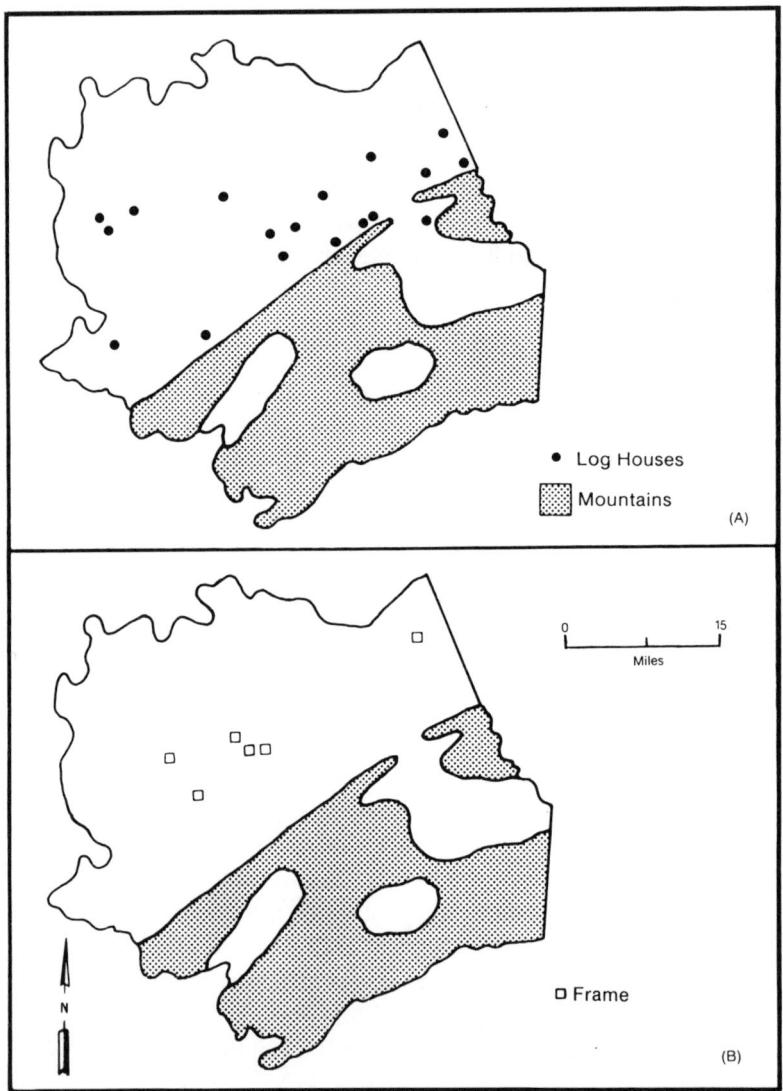

Map 5. Distribution of Blount county houses constructed during the 1860s and existing in 1984.

many frame houses as log structures may have been built. Of the extant houses, 49 of 88 (56 percent) were log, and 39 (44 percent) were frame structures (fig. 17). Although log houses were still dominant in farm areas, it is doubtful that they were being built in the towns or villages during that time. In fact, houses constructed in towns and villages make up 26 percent of the extant frame houses constructed during the decade.

The pattern of house construction in Blount County seems to conform to J.B. Killebrew's assessment of farm buildings in neighboring and more urban Knox County in 1874: "These generally are built of wood. The dwelling-houses often are of plank, but most generally of logs. They are neither handsome, comfortable, nor convenient, as compared with the better class of houses."[5] The comments of government official Thomas I. Saunders allow one to generalize about the dominance of log houses in rural Blount County in the 1870s. In early 1880, he wrote that the "farms are remarkably well enclosed, worm fencing being used almost exclusively, but the houses, as a general rule, are very indifferent log structures."[6]

The decline of house construction in the war-torn 1860s was reversed in the 1870s. The maps of the surviving log and frame houses show that many communities of the county today contain houses erected during the 1870s (map 6). The maps also reveal a continuation of the pre–Civil War geographical pattern of log and frame house construction. As indicated by the distribution of surviving log structures, log houses were erected throughout most of the county. Although the pattern of frame house construction appears to have become more dispersed than before the Civil War, there remained in the 1870s large areas with little or no frame construction. The remaining frame houses dating to the 1870s are concentrated primarily in the northern part of the county, as well as along the Little River and in the town of Maryville.

The decade of the 1880s is the first in which more frame than log houses were built in Blount County. Saunders' statement in-

52 ■ The Log House in East Tennessee

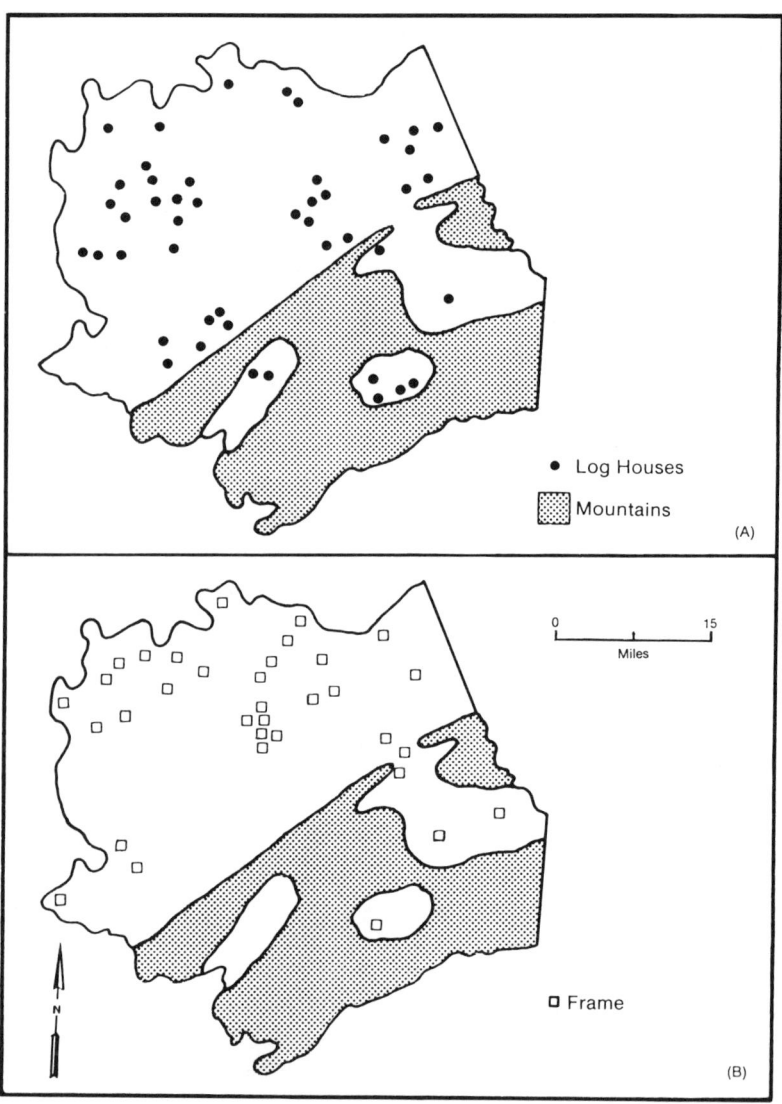

Map 6. Distribution of Blount County houses constructed during the 1870s and existing in 1984.

dicates that at the beginning of the decade the log house was the common dwelling type (fig. 21).[7] The historic building survey shows, however, that, based on number of existing structures, frame houses accounted for up to 70 percent of the residences erected during the 1880s (fig. 22). All except two of the nonlog houses were frame structures (fig. 17). It is possible, and perhaps probable, that more log houses from the 1880s have been destroyed than have frame houses built during that period. Even if that is the case, it is highly unlikely that differential rates of destruction could offset the overwhelming numerical predominance of frame houses.

Distribution maps of surviving log and frame houses reveal different geographical patterns for houses built in the 1880s than for those built in the 1870s (map 7). The distribution of frame houses in the 1880s is much more widespread than in the 1870s. In the 1980s, most areas in the county contained houses built in the 1880s, indicating that frame construction probably had diffused through nearly all of the county by the end of the decade. The distribution of log houses in the 1880s was concentrated especially in Tuckaleechee and Miller coves, and in the valleys along the west side of Chilhowee Mountain. Several log dwellings also were erected in the knobby and ridge areas west of Maryville, in the northwestern part of the county (fig.1).

Evidence that the late 1880s were dominated by frame rather than log construction in at least one area of the county is supplied by J.E. Prater. Prater, born in 1881, described conditions of the late 1880s in the Louisville area with remarkable clarity. He recalled the presence of several log houses in the Louisville area during his youth, but did not remember one log house being built in the area. He was, however, able to describe the construction of several frame houses in the area during the late 1880s and early 1890s.[8]

Maryville newspapers indicate that there was a great increase in house building in Blount County during the 1880s. In 1883, two newspapers reported that Maryville was undergoing a building boom.[9] The building activity apparently continued for several

Fig. 21. Single-pen log house of the 1870s (Blount County, 1984).

Fig. 22. Frame "I" house of the 1880s (Blount County, 1982).

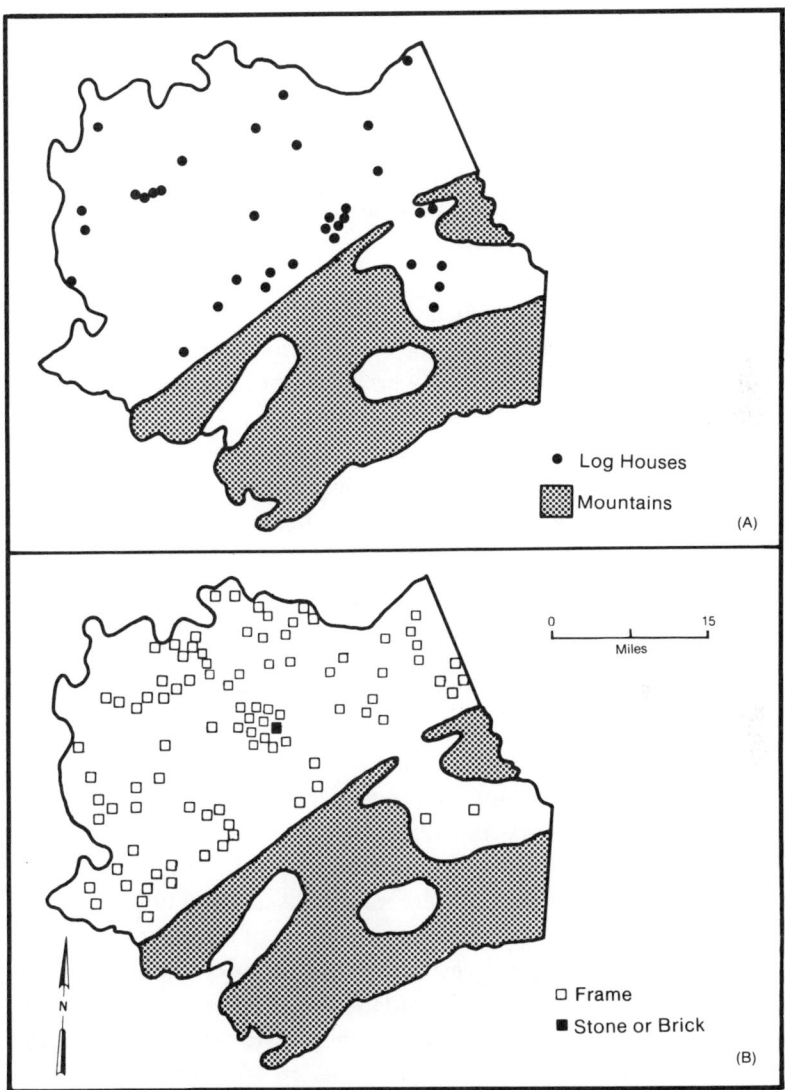

Map 7. Distribution of Blount County houses constructed during the 1880s and existing in 1984.

years. In May 1886, the *Maryville Times* quoted the *Knoxville Journal* as stating that Blount County had "shown more enterprise and push in the way of manufacturing and building in the past three years than it did for twenty before that."[10] The *Maryville Times* reported in early 1889 that at least two hundred buildings had been constructed in the town during the last three years.[11] Villages also experienced increased building activity in the middle and late 1880s, with Friendsville alone adding seven buildings in late 1889.[12]

During the middle and late 1880s, the rural sections of the county also were experiencing significant increases in the construction of residences. Nearly every issue of the *Maryville Times* contained local news reports from correspondents representing the various communities of the county. Many of the local reports contained references to building activities, and nearly every paper mentioned the construction of one or more houses in some section of the county. For example, in February 1886, three dwellings were to be "erected in the near future" at Clover Hill, a crossroads settlement southwest of Maryville.[13] Rural building activity seemed especially brisk during 1889. In August, the Twelfth District of the county, a few miles northeast of Maryville, was reported to be "on a boom, in building."[14] In November the Huffstettlers community, several miles south of Maryville, was undergoing "a boom in the way of building new residences."[15]

According to Maryville newspapers of the 1890s, the brisk building trend of the 1880s continued without interruption into the next decade. For example, new houses were being built in the Big Gully and Gamble's Store sections of the county in April 1890, and in early 1891, residences were under construction in the Waters, Miser Station, and Seaton communities.[16] It was reported in May 1892 that "some pretty residences have recently been erected" in the Ellejoy area, and in 1894 houses were reported built in several sections of the county, including Friendsville, Notime, Seaton, Tuckaleechee, Allegheny, and Cliff, where new buildings were being erected in November 1894.[17]

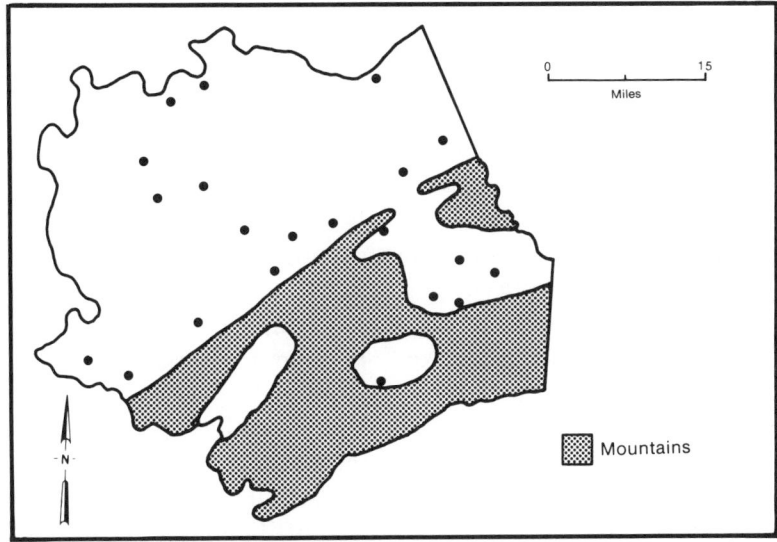

Map 8. Distribution of Blount County log houses constructed during the 1890s and existing in 1984.

The great majority of the houses built in Blount County during the 1890s were frame structures, and the degree of dominance of frame structures increased significantly over the previous decade. Of 219 houses built during the 1890s and still in existence in 1984, only 21 (9.5 percent) were log structures (fig. 17). Thirty-eight (17 percent) of the houses were erected in towns and villages, and all were nonlog structures, almost all frame. When town and village houses are excluded, the proportion of log houses built in the 1890s increased to 11.6 percent of the total built outside the nucleated settlements. The map of surviving 1890s log dwellings reflects the decline in overall numbers of log structures, and also shows that, as in the 1880s, most of the log houses were scattered through the mountain coves and the more isolated valleys in the area west of Chilhowee Mountain (Map 8).

Besides J.E. Prater, other elderly residents of Blount County suggested the accuracy of survey data. James T. Gamble, born in

1889, recalled in 1984 that several log barns were erected in the Wildwood area during the mid- and late 1890s, but he could not remember construction of any log dwellings.[18] The areas in which Prater and Gamble grew up had had a tradition of frame houses for several years prior to the 1890s, so it is not surprising that neither informant was aware of log house construction in his neighborhood.

An examination of house construction data indicates that the demise of log dwelling construction had occurred by the turn of the century (fig. 17). Of 327 existing Blount County houses built between about 1900 and 1905, only about 1 percent were log structures.

Data from the historic buildings survey indicates that the majority of houses built in Blount County prior to 1880 were log structures. This finding is compatible with the observation of Saunders, who in 1880 reported that most Blount County houses were log buildings. The 1880s were the first decade in which more frame than log dwellings were erected, and in the 1890s the dominance of frame construction increased to about 90 percent of all houses built. By the turn of the century, log dwellings were seldom erected.

The decline and virtual demise of log construction in Blount County, then, occurred quite rapidly. We may surmise that such a rapid shift in the method of house construction in an area reflected other significant changes in the area's economy and culture. For the moment, however, we shall defer consideration of these shifts and turn our attention to the ways in which log house construction was favored by certain conditions in East Tennessee in the nineteenth century.

CHAPTER FIVE

Persistence of Log House Construction

The persistence of log house construction in Blount County and East Tennessee until the late nineteenth century reflects a cultural tradition of the area's residents. Most of the nineteenth-century log houses were not built as temporary structures to be replaced shortly after construction by more substantial frame or brick buildings. On the contrary, the houses were generally well-constructed permanent buildings. Frame construction was another tradition in the eastern United States, and many frame dwellings were erected in antebellum East Tennessee, including several in Blount County. Some of East Tennessee's log house dwellers would have preferred to live in frame houses but were unable to do so. Whether one preferred to live in a frame or log house, there were certain conditions that favored log over frame construction. This chapter focuses on conditions that gave log construction advantages over frame construction in Blount County during the nineteenth century.

Timber Availability

Throughout the period of log house construction, rural Blount County had abundant timber resources, and it is likely that nearly every farm had enough timber to build a log house. Although there is a paucity of historical information on Blount County's timber resources, a few observers indicated that the county was still well endowed with timber after the Civil War.

In the early 1870s, J.B. Killebrew, secretary of the Tennessee Bureau of Agriculture, described the status of timber in Blount County:

> The county everywhere is well supplied with timber, though not always of the best quality, for fencing. On the upland, the black oak predominates, while hickory, post oak, white oak and yellow pine are abundant, the latter of a superior quality for building purposes. Along the streams may be found walnut, wild cherry, ash, and poplar; on the ridges the chestnut, and along the mountains the white, yellow and spruce pine, locust, all varieties of oak, poplars of enormous size, and forests of chestnut.

Later, in 1882, an observer stated that timber in Blount County was abundant, "consisting of pine, hickory, oak, ash, sweet gum, walnut, poplar, beech, &c."[2] In the same year a Maryville newspaper reported, "In every part of the county timber is to be found in abundance, oak and pine being the most plentiful: yet in certain localities poplar, walnut, hickory, chestnut, wild cherry and locust abound."[3]

Economy and Ease of Log Construction

The expense of log house construction was minimal because timber was available on the farm, labor was supplied by family members and neighbors, and few construction materials had to be purchased. A farmer, with one or two helpers and work animals, could remove the required number of logs from his woods, and they could cut and hew the logs to the desired lengths and widths. The construction of the log pen, however, required the labor of several more men and was usually a cooperative effort on the part of the farmer and his neighbors.

Such a "house raising" was described by George Brewer, who

observed the construction of log buildings in Coosa County, Alabama. His description is believed to be applicable to log house construction typical in Blount County during much of the nineteenth century:

> When the logs for a house were cut and put on the ground near where the house was to be built the neighbors were invited to come to the house raising on a specified day. They would assemble by seven or eight o'clock, and after the sills had been properly placed on their pillars of sawed lightwood blocks, or rocks, four men, skillful with an axe, were chosen as corner men, and each took possession of a corner ... The other men brought the logs and hoisted them to the corner men who would proceed at once to cutting a notch so as to fit the log below after the first had been fitted to the sill, so as to keep the wall both perpendicular and steady. Often a good fit would be secured at the first cutting. If not, the corner men turned the log up, remoddled [sic] the notch until a fit was secured. These men had for scaffolding on which to stand while cutting and fitting these notches only the cracks between the logs, or ... [the] top of the turned up log ... usually by night the house would be raised and the rafters (commonly skinned poles) were properly set upon the plates, as the flattened top log was called.[4]

Mary White, born in 1892 and a resident of the Rocky Branch section of Blount County, confirmed the tradition of house raisings in the county. When interviewed in 1982, she vividly recalled her grandfather's description of the construction of his log house, Mrs. White's residence, built in 1869. The house was raised in one day with the help of neighbors, and Mrs. White, without hesitation, recalled the names of the four cornermen and pointed out the corner that each manned while erecting the log pen.[5]

The cost of building a house was more expensive if a house carpenter was hired to supervise and participate in the operation. In Blount County, house carpenters were sometimes hired to build log dwellings, but if so, they usually, though not always, belonged to the more affluent farmers.[6] A good log pen, including the wall plates and rafters, could be erected in a single day with community help. The farmer was left with unfinished tasks such as chinking the spaces between the logs, putting boards on the roof and perhaps gables of the structure, and having a chimney constructed.

In sum, log construction was inexpensive and relatively easy. It would not seem to be an easy task, if one considers that individual logs weighed several hundred pounds, and some of them had to be lifted several feet high during the construction of a log wall. However, compared to the alternative—that is, the construction of a frame house—log house construction was fairly simple.

Difficulty in Obtaining Sawn Lumber

Difficulty in obtaining sawn lumber, because of lack of access to sawmills, was one of the most important reasons why residents of Blount County and other areas of the Upland South continued to build log houses decades after the initial settlement period. Before the Civil War, almost all the sawmills in Blount County and East Tennessee were water-powered mills, and their locations were limited to streams with flow adequate to turn a water wheel.[7]

Sawmills came into existence in Blount County with the beginning of permanent white settlement. They usually were built in conjunction with gristmills, but not all early gristmills were associated with sawmills. A gristmill is known to have existed in Blount County as early as 1788, but it is not known if a sawmill was present with the mill. At least five sawmills were in operation (with gristmills) in the county before 1800, and there may have been other sawmills at gristmill sites that were not specifically mentioned in early county records.[8] The five pre–1800 sawmills were Warner Martin's Mill on Nails Creek near Wildwood;

James McNutt's Mill on Pistol Creek in the present-day town of Alcoa; Andrew Kennedy's Mill on Little River near Wildwood; Samuel Shaw's Mill on Cloyd's Creek near Unitia; and Josiah Danforth's Mill on Pistol Creek in Maryville.[9] Several other sawmills are known to have been in operation before the Civil War, but the *Eighth Census of the United States* (1860) lists only six sawmills and eight sawmill employees for Blount County.[10] There were likely some sawmills not surveyed in the 1860 census, but even if several pre–Civil War sawmills were not mentioned, it is apparent that most residents of the county were not well served by sawmills during the first half of the nineteenth century.

Antebellum sawmills in Blount County engaged in custom sawing. Sawmill personnel did not go out in the community to bring logs to the mill. A farmer "snaked" logs from his woodland and transported them to the nearest mill, where the logs then were sawn into boards. The transportation of logs only a short distance to a mill was a difficult task for a farmer, who in most cases did not have adequate equipment to convey logs easily to the mill. Even softwood logs of reasonable length weighed several hundred pounds each, and to build a frame house, several such logs would have to be transferred to the mill and the lumber transported back by wagon or sled.

In addition to problems caused by poor access to sawmills before the Civil War, the nature of water-powered sawmills presented another problem—they were very slow. Water-powered sawmills of Blount County used the sash saw (also called the up-and-down saw), which was "mounted vertically in a frame." The saw frame was connected to a water wheel by a series of belts, pulleys, and wooden gears. As the up-and-down saw "made its cut, the log was carried along on a carriage regulated by a hand-operated ratchet." After the "length of the log had been sawn," the carriage was returned to its original position, the log realigned, and the process repeated.[11] Cutting capacity of sash sawmills was low and varied considerably with the amount of water flow. Early Appalachian sash mills had a capacity of approximately five hundred linear feet per day, no more than one-sixth the capacity of early steam-powered circular sawmills.[12]

In 1916 William B. Lenoir wrote a history of the Sweetwater Valley, located around the town of Sweetwater in adjacent Monroe County.[13] In describing conditions in the 1820s, Lenoir stated that "there were no saw mills except those using the up and down straight saw; consequently most of the houses first built were of hewed logs and in many instances floors of puncheons."[14] Lenoir did not bother to explain why one built a log house if only sash sawmills were present. Writing in 1916, he probably felt no need to explain the obvious—if one lived even a moderate distance away from a water-powered mill, one generally built a log house rather than confront the transportation problems inherent in frame house construction.

Poor access to sawmills did not mean that a farmer could not obtain some lumber for house construction. Most log houses used boards for roofing and to cover the gable ends of the structure. In addition, inside walls sometimes were lined with sawn planks. Roof boards and sometimes gable boards, which were only a few feet in length, were split by farmers with a club and a froe, but longer boards had to be sawed. Some farmers relied on sawmills for lumber, but others sawed the lumber on their farms with a whip saw or pit saw.[15] Whip-sawing or pit-sawing required two men to saw a log into boards by pulling a rip saw by hand. A log was laid on a platform beneath which was a pit. The saw was moved vertically by one man in the pit and another above the log on the platform, but the saw cut only on the downward stroke.[16] Whip sawing was such a difficult, slow process that two men could saw only "about 100 linear feet of plank in one day of back breaking toil."[17]

The extent to which the whip saw was used in Blount County is not known, but probably it was common. Burns stated that the Peter Brickey log house in Tuckaleechee Cove had whip-sawed rafters.[18] Its use in other parts of East Tennessee and Appalachia has been reported. In the mountains of neighboring Monroe

County, John Stratton used a whip saw to saw boards from logs to panel the inside walls of a log house built in 1839.[19] Later, in 1852, the Stratton family whip-sawed a coffin for a visiting relative who died at the Stratton home.[20]

Some Blount County residents either did not perceive a need for sawn lumber or were unable to obtain it. These people built their houses completely of logs, including the gable ends, through the use of the ridgepole-and-purlin roof. Such a roof had a round log ridgepole and a series of round log purlins, all running parallel to the front of the structure, to support the roof cover. The Elijah Hatcher house, built in the 1830s in West Millers Cove, and the Elijah Oliver house, built in the 1870s in Cades Cove, were erected with logs in the gable ends of the buildings (fig. 23). Numerous outbuildings were constructed in Cades Cove with log gable ends. The advantage of using logs up to the apex of the structure was that neither sawn lumber nor nails were required for the construction of a log pen. These existing structures with log gable ends are found in some of the more isolated sections of the county. Their presence illustrates that it was difficult for some farmers to obtain even small amounts of sawmill lumber during much of the nineteenth century.

Frame Construction Before 1860

Even if a farmer obtained sawn lumber it was not easy to build a frame house during the first half of the nineteenth century. The type of frame construction prevalent in East Tennessee was timber frame construction, sometimes referred to as post-and-beam or braced-frame construction.[21] The timber frame consisted of a series of substantial wall posts and beams supported by braces (fig. 24).

In many of the early East Tennessee timber frame houses, all the members—corner posts, plates, studs, and braces—were hand hewn. Even if the members were sawn by a sash sawmill or a whip saw and hewing was not required, the construction of the

Fig. 23. Elijah Oliver log house in Cades Cove, Blount County (1984). Side view of larger front pen shows gable-end logs extending to the apex of the structure and reveals the ends of the ridgepole-and-purlin roof logs. The smaller rear pen is an example of a detached kitchen unit, common in the Upland South during the nineteenth century.

timber frame presented difficulty. Expert carpentry skill was needed to erect the frame, because the posts, beams, braces, and studs were interconnected by mortises, tenons, and pegs (fig. 24). Even for a basic, not elegant timber frame house, the tasks of making mortises, tenons, and pegs and auguring pegholes were such that completion of a frame house usually was a rather long, involved process. Some of the older Blount County frame houses took more than a year to complete.

It is difficult today to determine the construction characteristics of old frame houses, because the frame normally is covered by exterior siding and interior paneling. Occasionally, however, the frame of an abandoned or dilapidated house is visible, and it is possible to determine the construction technique. In addition, sometimes one can discern some of the construction characteristics of a house by examining the structure from a base-

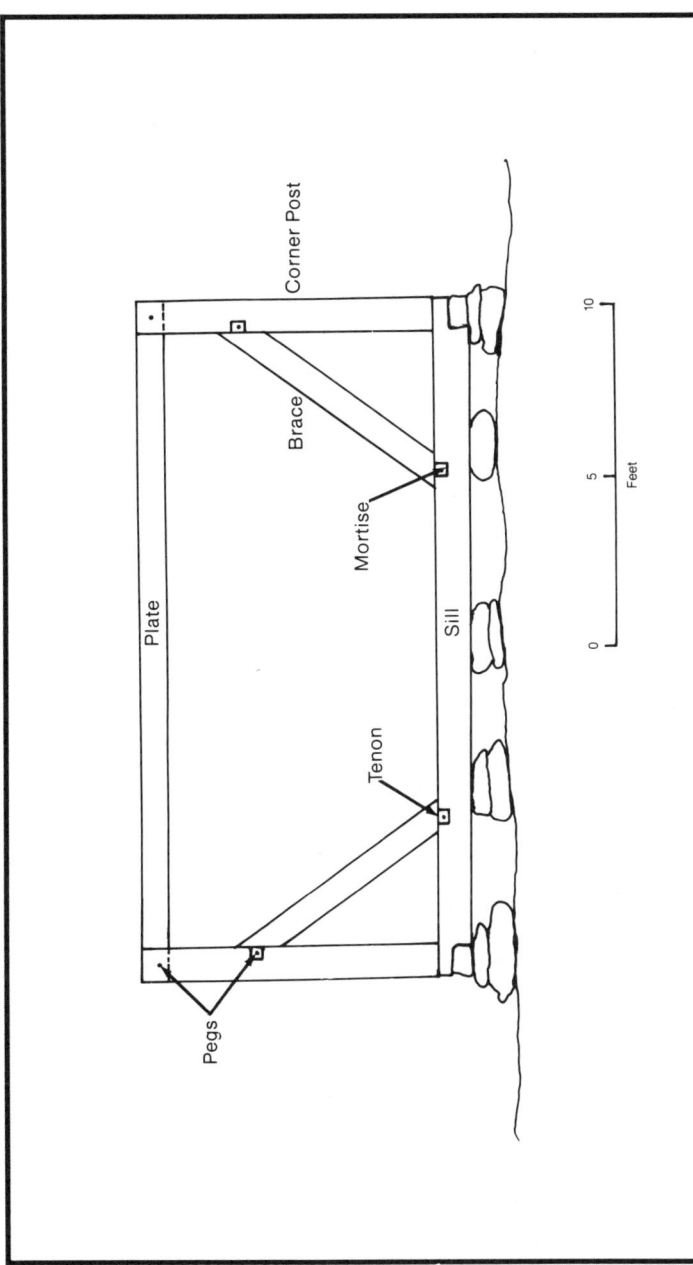

Fig. 24. Timber frame construction. Source: Modified from Kline, Pace, and Carnes, An Archeological Reconnaissance Survey of the Proposed Pigeon Forge Park, Sevier County, 14.

ment or an attic. For only very few pre–Civil War frame houses in Blount County was it possible to make a complete examination, but twenty-one were observed in enough detail to determine the construction type. All twenty-one of the buildings exhibited characteristics consistent with timber frame construction.

A detailed examination was made of the framing of two houses built in the area by 1800. One of the houses, the Samuel Wear house (c. 1800), located in Sevier County, was investigated just prior to its destruction. The other, the Warner Martin house (c. 1794), located along Nails Creek near Wildwood, is believed to be the oldest frame house existing in Blount County at the time of writing (fig. 19). Both of these houses exhibited characteristics typical of timber frame construction. They had corner posts tenoned and pegged into mortised sills and plates; the posts, sills, and plates were supported by connecting tenoned and pegged braces; studs were tenoned into sills and plates; floor and ceiling joists were notched into mortises of sills and plates. No nails were used to support or connect any of the elements of the frame. All members of the Wear house were hand hewn, whereas some of the members of the Martin house were sash sawn. The presence of sawn members was not surprising, because Warner Marter had a combination grist and sawmill on his farm as early as c. 1793. Both the corner posts were L-shaped, and each post on the Wear house was one piece of wood, hewn to the desired L shape.[22]

Examination of the Ira Peery house, built c. 1850, and the Peter Brakebill house, built in 1855, revealed both structures to have timber frame construction. Corner posts were hand hewn and connected by mortise, tenon, and peg to the plates and sills. Braces, however, were nailed to the posts, sills, and plates. Studs were nailed to the sills and plates on the Brakebill house but were mortised and tenoned in the Peery house. All the members of the Peery and Brakebill houses were sawed except for the posts and sills, which were hewed by hand. The floor joists of the Brakebill house were sash-sawn 2x10s and 3x10s, whereas those in the Peery house were large round logs, slightly hewn on top.

If the Peery and Brakebill houses were indicative of dwellings built in the 1850s, it can be stated that frame house construction had not changed significantly during the previous fifty years. The greatest change discerned during that period was the shift to the use of nails to hold braces in place. Frame house construction during the antebellum period in Blount County can be characterized as timber frame construction, requiring expert carpentry skills for its completion. Patrick described the skill required of Tennessee carpenters in constructing a timber frame house:

> The skill house carpenters brought to their work was the ability to cut and carve chimney pieces, doors, and moldings and to join wood to wood with mortises, tenons, and pegs in house frames, trusses, and paneling. Each frame house was the work of carpenters who let each stud into the sill and plate, set the corner posts and braces, and attached each piece of weatherboarding to the studs with pegs.[23]

There were few carpenters in early East Tennessee, even in the larger towns. The state capital of Knoxville had only five carpenters in 1801, and it can be assumed that there were proportionally fewer carpenters in rural areas around Knoxville at that time.[24] Rural areas in Blount County probably were not well served by carpenters before the Civil War. As late as 1870, there were only thirty-five carpenters in the county; at least fourteen and perhaps as many as nineteen of those were located in Maryville (table 3).[25] Most rural communities had only one or two carpenters and several, such as Cades Cove, Tuckaleechee, and Chilhowee, had none listed in the 1870 census manuscript returns.[26] It is possible that some carpenters were also farmers, and appear in the census with "farmer" as occupation rather than "carpenter." It is difficult, if not impossible, to determine to what extent the demand for carpenters was being met in nineteenth-century Blount County. It appears, however, that there was a shortage of carpenters in the rural sections of the county, and any shortage of house carpenters would make it likely that more farmers would opt to build log houses.

An additional factor that might influence the decision to build a log house was the availability and price of nails during the pre–Civil War period. Before the 1700s, only hand-wrought nails were available in this country. Cut nail machines came into use during the late 1700s but probably were not widely distributed until the early nineteenth century.[27]

Little is known about the production and distribution of nails in early East Tennessee, but soon after 1800, nails were being made by one of the Embree brothers (Elihu or Elijah) in Washington County.[28] Elijah Embree apparently became the principal supplier of nails for all of East Tennessee. In 1834, Eastin Morris wrote in *The Tennessee Gazeteer* that Embree's nail factory "supplied nearly the whole country east of Huntsville, Alabama with first rate nails."[29]

Nails certainly were available in the towns of East Tennessee by the 1830s. An advertisement in the *Knoxville Register* in April 1834 announced that Robert King had "just received for sale, on the usual terms—forty seven kegs Embree's Nails assorted."[30] The supply of nails appears to have increased by the early 1840s, when Knoxville merchants advertised "Eastern" and "Tennessee" nails.[31] By 1850, nails in varied sizes were available in Knoxville and Maryville stores. The *Knoxville Register* in June 1850 carried an advertisement for merchant C. Wallace, informing readers that a large consignment of Eastern and Tennessee nails, of all sizes, had been received.[32] In 1855, Toole's Hardware in Maryville reported the receipt of "20 kegs best Eastern nails, for sale cheap,"[33] and in 1857 T.J. and C. Powell of Knoxville advertised a stock of two hundred kegs of nails "assorted from 3 to 40."[34] It is not known, however, to what extent neighborhood stores, removed from the towns, carried nails during the pre–Civil War period.

Nail prices decreased significantly during the 1840s. In Knox-

Table 3
Number and Distribution of Carpenters in Blount County, 1870

District	Post Office	No. of Families in District	No. of Carpenters in District
1	Morganton	158	0
	Brick Mill		
2	Morganton	135	1
3	Morganton	145	2
	Coyte		
	Unitia		
4	Unitia	159	3
	Friendsville		
5	Friendsville	145	2
	Miser Station		
6	Clover Hill	138	2
7	Maryville	125	5
	Montvale Springs		
8	Maryville	144	1
9	Maryville	303	14
10	Louisville	189	2
11	Rockford	156	1
12	Maryville	115	1
13	Ellejoy	183	0
14	Gamble's Store	174	1
15	Tuckaleechee	186	0
16	Cades Cove	66	0
17	Chilhowee	86	0
		2607	35

Source: Ninth Census of the United States (1870), Manuscript Schedules for Blount County.

ville, Eastern nails sold for ten to ten-and-a-half cents per pound in 1841, and Tennessee nails for nine-and-a-half cents per pound.[35] By 1849, Eastern nails were sold for seven-and-a-half cents per pound and Tennessee nails for six-and-a-half cents per pound.[36]

It is difficult to determine what role the availability and price of nails played in the decision of a farmer to build a particular kind of house in antebellum Blount County. It appears that by the 1830s nail supply was not a problem in East Tennessee and Blount County. The price of nails, however, may have discouraged some farmers from building frame houses.

The Traditional Economy

The economy that developed in East Tennessee during the nineteenth century contributed to the dominance of the log house in the area. By 1840, East Tennessee had emerged from the frontier period, but conditions did not change there to the extent that they did in Middle and West Tennessee, where commercial agriculture developed significantly during the late antebellum period.[37] A self-sufficient agricultural economy persisted in East Tennessee, and most of the region's inhabitants were non-slave holding yeoman farmers who worked small farms with their families. They had very little money but were not destitute; they produced nearly everything they consumed and did not lack the basic necessities of life.[38] However, such an economy probably did not generate the capital required to purchase construction materials for a frame house or to hire a house carpenter to build the structure.

According to historian Blanche H. Clark, East Tennessee did not develop commercial agriculture to a great extent, because of problems with poor soils, topography, and inaccessibility to markets. The mountains of East Tennessee had thin soils but contained much timber, and wild grasses were abundant enough in the mountains to allow for the development of stock grazing. The valleys of East Tennessee had fertile soils and produced general crops, especially grains such as corn, wheat, and oats.[39] Geographer Donald W. Buckwalter has concluded that the primary constraint on the development of commercial agriculture in antebellum East Tennessee was not environmental conditions but a transportation disadvantage relative to neighboring regions.[40]

In 1850 and 1860, about 60 percent of East Tennessee farmers owned their land, the rest being tenants, sharecroppers, day laborers, and squatters.[41] Historians Owsley and Owsley attempted to explain why 40 percent of East Tennessee's farmers failed to own land in 1850 and 1860, when large amounts of public land were available in East Tennessee. The Owsleys believed that many of the nonowners were renters who preferred to rent good valley lands rather than buy and have to improve more marginal lands. Some renters also had family ties with their landlords; they may have rented from their parents, a father-in-law, or an uncle. Many of the farmers who are classed as squatters may have been in the process of acquiring the lands they occupied.[42] The fact that 40 percent of East Tennessee farmers were landless had an effect on house-building patterns in the area, because it is unlikely that one who did not own land would build a frame house.

According to contemporary observers, economic conditions in East Tennessee during the 1870s did not differ greatly from conditions during antebellum days. Killebrew characterized the great majority of East Tennessee farmers in the 1870s as small farmers owning one hundred to two hundred acres of land and working the fields themselves. They produced little for commercial sale but made a great effort to produce nearly all the commodities required for home consumption.[43] Killebrew described the typical self-sufficient farm of East Tennessee:

> It is not uncommon on a small farm to see a patch of cotton, which the women of the household work into cloth; a spot given to tobacco for home consumption; a field of sorghum from which syrup is made for domestic use; a few acres of wheat are raised for flour; corn and oats or hay to feed the stock, which usually consist of a few sheep to supply wool for winter clothes, cows from which a considerable revenue is derived by the manufacture of butter, and a brood-mare or two from which the farmer rears his mules and horses for farm use. Besides these, an abundance of the standard vegetables, such as cabbage, beans, peas, potatoes and onions, is raised, as well as of ducks, chickens, geese, guinea-fowls, peafowls, &c.

A few bee-hives, and an apple and peach orchard, are the necessary adjuncts to nine-tenths of the farms in East Tennessee. The most striking fact in the farming operations of that division, is that no money crop, so-called, is raised. Tobacco, cotton, corn and hay are all grown in small quantities, not so much for sale as for use.[44]

Most farmers did purchase a few commodities not produced on their farms—primarily salt, coffee, and sugar—from neighborhood stores. Such purchases were generally not paid for with cash, but through a barter system in which feathers, eggs, chickens, dried fruit, butter, and other items produced on the farm were traded for the desired store commodities.[45] Evidence of the persistence of the barter system is seen in East Tennessee newspaper advertisements during the 1870s. [The] *Maryville Republican* of 26 February 1870, for example, carried several advertisements offering goods to readers in exchange for cash or farm commodities.[46] Edmund Cody Burnett, recalling his youth in Cocke County, Tennessee, suggested the pervasiveness of the barter system:

> The shingle makers sold their shingles to the Big Creek storekeepers and took in exchange such good as they desired or were obtainable. Cash transactions were almost unknown. Money was so scarce that even the fairly well-to-do often had difficulty in paying their taxes. Almost the entire business of the stores was done by barter . . . The shingle maker purchased on credit and later paid the account in shingles, sometimes supplemented by eggs, feathers, and chickens.[47]

The self-sufficient economy described above was dominant in Blount County for much of the nineteenth century. Saunders indicated that the traditional way of life in Blount County persisted in 1880. He stated that the people "dress plainly, go to church regularly; and deal honestly with each other. They live on farms; their sons inherit and live there after them, and the tendency is for one generation to assume and perpetuate the habits of that immediately preceding it. The spinning wheel and the loom are seen in their houses, however well-to-do they may be."[48]

A. Randolph Shields, who grew up in the mountains of Blount County, has written an excellent account of self-sufficient living in his native Cades Cove.[49] The characteristics of rural life in Cades Cove, as described by Shields, are believed to be typical of life in most interior parts of Blount County during the past century. According to Shields:

> Each family provided for its own needs. Separated from the main American marketplace, people here had little use for cash in the day-to-day life of the cove. They depended upon themselves and their neighbors for the food and few comforts they enjoyed. Each person in the family, young and old alike, shared in maintaining the household. Work was central to the family life of these mountain people.[50]

Although most antebellum Blount County farms were self-sufficient units that did not produce large surpluses for market, most had some degree of commercial orientation. Cades Cove farmers, including those with small holdings, were able to sell crops from their mountain cove in the Knoxville market, because farmers engaged in cooperative or shared transportation of commodities. A few farmers, especially valley farmers living along the Tennessee and lower Little rivers, operated relatively large farms producing considerable surpluses for off-farm sale. These valley farms, some of which could be considered plantations, were different from the yeoman farms of the county; as Killebrew noted, they "resemble[d] the best farms of Middle Tennessee."[51]

Much of the commercial activity centered on the town of Louisville, a port on the Tennessee River.[52] Louisville became an important port after 1828, when steamboat navigation developed on the river. From about 1835 until the Civil War, Louisville was the dominant economic center in Blount County, as river transportation provided the area with access to Alabama markets, as well as to faraway markets such as New Orleans.[53]

Wheat raising and livestock grazing were the most important commercial agricultural activities in East Tennessee before the Civil War. Historian Lewis Cecil Gray stressed the manner in which wheat's importance as a commercial crop in the 1850s was enhanced by railroad construction: "It was the principal market crop of east Tennessee, which enjoyed a limited market for its flour in northern Alabama . . . The extension of railway lines from the coast to Knoxville and building of the Nashville and Chattanooga Railroad made it possible to transport the grain to coastal cities that had hitherto imported from the North."[54] The advantage of livestock production over other activities, especially in areas without access to rail or water transportation, was the ability of the animals to transport themselves to market. Livestock droving allowed East Tennessee to supply meat to areas east and south, including Piedmont plantation areas and the Tennessee Valley of Alabama.[55]

Many valley farmers differed from yeomen farmers not only in agricultural production patterns but also in the types of houses they occupied. From the late eighteenth and to the mid-nineteenth century, the great majority of farmers in Blount County lived in log houses, which varied from small one-room, one-story structures to large two-story buildings with several rooms. As commercial activities began to develop and some farmers began to prosper, especially during the 1840s and 1850s, the affluent ones began to build frame and sometimes brick houses.

The pre–Civil War frame and brick houses were associated especially with the relatively wealthy valley farmers who lived close to the Tennessee River. Some valley farmers, however, continued to live in log houses until after the Civil War. It can be concluded that log dwellers represented all segments of the farm community, from the wealthy to the landless, whereas frame and brick dwellings were associated only with a select group of farmers, town dwellers, or others with access to sawmills.

Table 4
Value of Real Estate and Personal Property for Frame and Brick House Dwellers in Blount County in 1860

Name	Occupation	Value of Real Estate in Dollars	Value of Personal Property in Dollars
Thos. McCullough	Farmer	$10,000	$ 2,300
Richard Kirby	Farmer	5,000	7,000
Sally Martin	Farmer	5,000	7,500
Stephen S. Porter	Farmer	25,300	16,750
Jas. Porter	Farmer	20,000	10,000
Alex. McNutt	Farmer	15,000	10,000
Robert Pickens	Farmer	3,500	3,700
J.S. George	Farmer	18,000	18,000
		Mean: 12,725	Mean: 9,406

Source: Eighth Census of the United States (1860), Manuscript Schedules of Population for Blount County.

This conclusion is supported by data from the Eighth U.S. Census (1860). Heads of families who lived in frame and brick houses owned real estate and personal property valued at considerably more than the average figures for heads of families living in log houses (tables 4 and 5). The data also show that among log house dwellers were not only yeomen farmers with moderate wealth, but also the relatively wealthy and the poor.

In sum, most of the houses built in Blount County before 1880 were log structures, and during the era of log construction, certain conditions existed that gave log construction advantages over frame construction. Those conditions included an abundance of timber for log construction; low cost and ease of log construction compared to frame construction; poor access to sawmills and lumber; and the self-sufficient economy of the area. It was necessary for some of the conditions described in this chapter to change before log construction would be replaced by frame construction. The next three chapters will ex-

Table 5
Value of Real Estate and Personal Property for Log House Dwellers in Blount County in 1860

Name	Occupation	Value of Real Estate in Dollars	Value of Personal Property in Dollars
Archibald Hitch	Farmer	$2,000	$ 200
Alexander Duncan	Farmer	5,000	3,000
Thomas Clark	Farmer	4,000	4,000
Edward Wilkerson	Farmer	1,500	4,500
Newton McConnell	Farmer	1,500	1,200
James Grindstaff	Farmer	2,000	450
Alfred McConnell	Farmer	8,000	4,600
Daniel Headrick	Farmer	3,000	1,200
Robt. Everett	Farmer	800	350
James Waters	Farmer	3,000	1,200
Josiah Gamble	Farmer	5,000	1,000
Jacob Tipton	Farmer	600	1,000
Eli Garner	Farmer	500	1,000
Asa Rogers	Farmer	1,500	550
Jesse Milsaps	Tenant	0	500
Aaron Burns	Tenant	0	800
Elija Hatcher	Farmer	2,500	1,500
Sam Lane	Farmer	400	225
Richard Burns	Farmer	2,000	2,500
Elija Oliver	Farmer	500	340
John Oliver	Farmer	500	500
Peter Cable	Farmer	1,200	1,225
Daniel Losson	Farmer	2,000	1,600
		Mean: 2,065	Mean: 1,454

Source: Eighth Census of the United States (1860), Manuscript Schedules of Population for Blount County.

amine conditions in Blount County during the latter half of the nineteenth century, to determine the relations between the decline in log construction and social, economic, and technological change.

CHAPTER SIX

Socioeconomic Factors and the Decline of Log House Construction

Pre–Civil War frame and brick houses were associated with relatively wealthy Blount County farmers who were probably more commercially oriented than other farmers. It is logical to hypothesize that the shift from log to frame construction during the latter part of the nineteenth century was associated with increased wealth gained by farmers who had begun to produce greater surpluses for off-farm sale than in the past. If farmers were more commercially oriented, they would accumulate more money, some of which could be used to pay for the construction of frame houses.

An examination of U.S. Census of Agriculture data does not indicate that agricultural production at the turn of the century was significantly greater than during the antebellum period. There was an absolute increase in the number of improved acres of agricultural land between 1850 and 1900, but with an increase in number of farms, there was a considerable decline in the number of improved acres per farm. Corn, wheat, and oats were the three traditional field crops of East Tennessee, but only wheat production had increased significantly by 1900. Wheat acreage per farm, however, declined between 1860 and 1900. Although livestock production was an important source of revenue for East

Tennessee farms in the nineteenth century, the total number of animals grown in Blount County decreased between 1860 and 1900.[1]

It appears that, rather than exhibiting great increases in agricultural production during the postwar period, Blount County at best began to approach pre–Civil War levels of production during the latter part of the century. The postbellum agricultural situation in Blount County appears to have paralleled that of the state as a whole, which "did not regain its losses nor reach its pre-Civil War level until 1900."[2] There was, however, considerable surplus production and commercial agricultural activity in Blount County after the Civil War, particularly from the late 1870s until the turn of the century. Saunders indicated in 1880 that Blount County farmers produced "enough to live on and a good deal to export." And according to Dunn, prosperity had returned to the agricultural economy of mountainous Cades Cove by the 1880s.[3]

Railroad construction may have stimulated the development of commercial agriculture in parts of Blount County during the latter half of the nineteenth century. A rail line connecting Maryville with Knoxville was completed in 1868, and another, running parallel to the Tennessee River through the western part of the county, was constructed in 1890.[4] These railroads connected Blount County with northern and southern markets and likely provided incentive for farmers with access to them to concentrate on crop production for off-farm sale. It is possible that some farmers accumulated enough money through newly-developed commercial agriculture to replace their log houses with frame structures.

The above statements are speculative, however, because the railroads may have brought about a shift from river to rail transportation of agricultural commodities, without causing an increase in overall agricultural production. Support for such an occurrence is provided by Blount Countian A.H. Love, who in 1922 indicated that the port of Louisville had suffered economic disaster as a result of railroad construction through the town: "The writer wishes again to touch on the shipping business on the river . . . great changes have taken place. The wharf and warehouses are gone; the steamboat business is a relic of the past . . . We have the railroad, but what benefit have we derived from its coming? We won't say the railroad caused it, but our town is not the town it once was by several hundred percent."⁵

Although agricultural production did not exceed pre–Civil War levels greatly, if at all, frame-house building increased tremendously. Not only did the affluent build frame houses as before the war, but many yeomen farmers built frame dwellings during the 1880s and 1890s, and relatively poor farmers were erecting frame residences in the 1890s. Commercial agriculture was responsible for the accumulation of capital needed to build some frame houses, but it was not responsible for the construction of frame dwellings by the general populace.

An examination of the manuscript returns of the Ninth U.S. Census in 1870 reveals certain differences between fourteen men identified in the Blount County building survey as frame-house builders during the 1870s and fourteen men identified as having erected log dwellings during that decade. Frame-house builders tended to be older and wealthier than log-house builders, although most of the frame-house builders were not as wealthy as their pre–Civil War counterparts (tables 6 and 7). Ages of log-house builders ranged from twenty-one to sixty-one years. Nine of the fourteen were in their twenties at the time of dwelling construction, and the group's average age was thirty-one years. The fourteen frame builders ranged in age from twenty-seven to fifty-four and had a mean age of thirty-seven at the time the structures were built (tables 6 and 7). Eight of the fourteen log builders were either tenant farmers or farm laborers in 1870, although they probably owned land at the time their houses were constructed. Three were not listed in the census, and two of those are known to have moved to the county after 1870. Two were landowning farmers, and the other was a minor, thirteen years old in 1870. Eight of the fourteen frame-house builders owned property, and another,

Table 6

Characteristics of Blount County Frame House Builders During the 1870s

	Construction Date	Age of Builder at Time of Construction	Occupation of Builder in 1870	Value of Builder's Real Estate in 1870 in Dollars	Value of Builder's Personal Property in 1870 in Dollars
1	c. 1878	28	Farm Laborer	---	---
2	c. 1870	38	House Carpenter	$1,000	$ 600
3	c. 1875	36	Farmer	500	150
4	1873	29	Farmer	8,000	2,423
5	1874–76	c. 33	Farm Laborer	---	---
6	1875–79	c. 30	Farmer	1,500	950
7	c. 1870	53	Farmer	350	300
8	c. 1875	40	Physician	---	---
9	1876	29	Farm Laborer	---	300
10	1874–76	c. 36	Farmer	4,000	500
11	c. 1877	54	Farmer	4,000	1,100
12	c. 1875	40	Wagon Maker	---	---
13	1875	27	Farm Laborer	---	---
14	c. 1870	40	Physician	3,000	1,500

Source: Ninth Census of the United States (1870), Manuscript Schedules of Population for Blount County.

Table 7

Characteristics of Blount County Log House Builders During the 1870s

	Construction Date	Age of Builder at Time of Construction	Occupation of Builder in 1870	Value of Builder's Real Estate in 1870 in Dollars	Value of Builder's Personal Property in 1870 in Dollars
1	1875	c. 32	Not Living In County	---	---
2	c. 1873	28	Tenant Farmer	---	$400
3	1870–75	c. 32	Tenant Farmer	---	---
4	c. 1875	26	Tenant Farmer	---	$300
5	c. 1873	26	Living With Parents; Probably Farm Laborer	---	---
6	1870–75	c. 24	Not Listed In 1870 Census	---	---
7	c. 1870	28	Tenant Farmer	---	---
8	1870–75	c. 27	Farm Laborer	---	$500
9	1870–75	c. 26	Farm Laborer	---	---
10	c. 1875	61	Not Living In County	---	---
11	1870–72	c. 26	Farm Laborer	---	---
12	c. 1878	c. 21	None, 13 Years Old	---	---
13	1870s	c. 45	Farmer	$800	$400
14	1876	34	Farmer	$300	$600

Source: Ninth Census of the United States (1870), Manuscript Schedules of Population for Blount County.

a physician, was probably relatively affluent at the time his frame house was erected. In addition, one of the builders was a landless wagon maker who had considerable personal property in 1870 (table 7).[6]

In the 1880s, differences in the ages of frame- and log-house builders became more pronounced than in the 1870s. The average age of thirty-one frame builders was thirty-six years, or about the same as during the 1870s. In addition to the thirty-one builders identified during the building survey, an examination of Blount County newspapers of the 1880s revealed the names of numerous house builders, all believed to have erected frame or brick dwellings. Ages were determined for twenty of those builders, the average being thirty-seven years, virtually the same as for the group previously identified. The average ages of twelve log-house builders, however, dropped to twenty-seven years, and nine of the twelve were younger than thirty years old at the time their residences were constructed.[7]

By the 1880s, non-affluent yeomen farmers were building frame houses. Field interviews and census information revealed that log houses were being erected in the 1880s by younger farmers, usually relatively poor and recently married. The log structures might be considered "starter" houses, to be enlarged, usually with a frame addition, as the farmer's family grew larger and as he accumulated more wealth.

Terry Jordan has attributed the decline of log construction in Texas at least partly to a social stigma. He stated that log dwellings "became symbols of the frontier, of backwardness, of deprivation," and that social status could be improved by "discarding the log house and replacing it with one of frame, brick, or stone," or by concealing the logs with siding.[8]

There is evidence that some East Tennesseans were not content to live in log dwellings. The Cobb-Massengill log house, built around 1770–72, served as the first capitol of the Territory of Tennessee. This structure remained virtually unchanged until the late nineteenth century. At that time, however, the daughters of owner William Allen Massengill had reached "courting age" and "were too embarrassed to live in a log house." The owner weatherboarded the house to allay his daughters' embarrassment.[9]

It can be assumed that some of the rural elite of Blount County, even during the pioneer period, were not content to live in log dwellings. Some of them built frame or brick houses as soon as they were able and abandoned their log structures. James Campbell McConnell built a two-story brick house near Meadow to replace a log house during the first decade of the nineteenth century.[10] James Henry, of the Brick Mill community, went to great effort to build an elegant two-story brick house, which replaced a log house in the early 1830s. Henry and his brother-in-law, carpenter Buck Lattimore, "took wood cutters and went by wagon to Virginia to secure patterns for the new house." Some of the wood used in constructing the house was sawed in Virginia and hauled to Blount County.[11]

Some members of the rural elite were unable to, or simply made no effort to, "escape" from their log houses for many years before the Civil War, and yeomen farmers apparently made little effort to build frame houses until after the Civil War. Killebrew, writing in 1874, lamented the poor status of housing in East Tennessee. In describing conditions in Sequatchie County, for example, he stated that there was "almost total neglect in removing the ancient houses erected by the early settlers, and building more desirable ones."[12]

It is possible that the writings of public officials such as Killebrew, who was secretary of the Tennessee Bureau of Agriculture, caused some people to feel that log houses were undesirable as living quarters. Local newspaper editors also may have influenced the attitudes of East Tennesseans during the period of decline in log house construction. One Blount County editor appears to have designated himself the county "change agent" for the 1880s. He was continually exhorting residents to make improvements to their property, apparently in an effort to make the county more attractive to outside investors. In one such appeal, he made it clear that log houses were not desirable, but might be tolerated if certain improvements were made: "Farmers, build nice fences around your homes, and if you can't paint them, whitewash them. Even log houses with good whitewashed fences gives homes a cheerful aspect, and that is what we want."[13]

The addition of numerous rural post offices and an increase in the frequency of mail delivery during the latter part of the nineteenth century made it easier for Blount Countians to learn about conditions outside the area. Twenty-four post offices were added in the county during the 1880s and sixteen during the 1890s.[14] The mail brought newspapers and magazines to even the most isolated parts of the county. Newspapers and magazines did not introduce frame houses to the general populace, because a few frame houses were present in nearly all communities by the 1880s. Illustrations of and advertisements for modern houses may have contributed, however, to the yeoman farmer's desire to build a frame house to replace a log residence.

It is difficult to assess to what extent a social stigma was experienced by most Blount Countians who lived in log dwellings. It seems reasonable to assume that there was such a stigma among the affluent before the Civil War, and that such an attitude was gradually adopted by the lower socioeconomic classes as more people built frame houses after the war. Even if there was a stigma associated with living in a log house, before the 1880s or 1890s, most families were unable to avoid it by building a frame house.

The shift from log to frame construction, then, was not indicative of a great increase in commercial agriculture in the county, nor was it associated only with relatively wealthy Blount Countians. In fact, by 1890, frame construction was employed by members of virtually all segments of rural society. Many Blount Countians may have considered it socially unacceptable to live in a log house by the end of the nineteenth century. If the typical Blount County farm family considered it demeaning to live in a log house, however, certain conditions had to change before most farmers erected frame houses.

CHAPTER SEVEN

Sawmilling and Lumbering and the Decline of Log House Building

In Blount County, the shift from log to frame construction between the 1870s and 1900 was associated with changes in sawmilling and the rise of commercial lumbering. The difficulty of obtaining sawn lumber before the 1870s resulted largely from lack of access to sawmills. Greater access to lumber was made possible by an increase in the number of sawmills in the county and by the advent of the portable sawmill. The changes in sawmilling, however, would not have occurred so rapidly without a significant increase in commercial lumbering.

The Role of Sawmills

Several authors have attributed the decline of log construction and the rise of frame construction to the diffusion of sawmills. Eller has stated that in Appalachia "frame houses were made increasingly feasible by the construction of neighborhood sawmills," and Zelinsky has asserted that "the multiplication of sawmills made frame construction feasible even for the poorest classes."[1] It is not possible to determine how many sawmills were operating in Blount County during the post–Civil War period because the Ninth and Tenth U.S. Censuses (1870 and 1880) probably understated the number of sawmills. In addition, census data on sawmills are missing from the 1890 and 1900 censuses. Killebrew provides evidence that there were more sawmills in Blount County than were reported by the censuses. According to the census data, there were nine sawmills in the county in 1870, and only eight in 1880.[2] Killebrew, however, reports that twenty-three mills were in operation in the early 1870s.[3]

Even though accurate sawmill numbers are not available, there is evidence that the number of Blount County sawmills increased greatly during the 1880s and 1890s, when the transition from log to frame construction was most pronounced. Data compiled from various sources, including censuses, newspapers, books, and journals, show that at least forty sawmills were in operation in the county during the 1880s. By 1897, the number had increased to at least fifty-two, and the distance rural residents had to travel to mills, to have logs converted to planks, had decreased considerably.[4] Thus the increase in number of sawmills almost certainly facilitated the construction of frame houses in the county.

More important than the absolute increase in number of sawmills in Blount County was the advent of the portable steam-powered circular sawmill, which by 1872 had "almost entirely superseded the reciprocating mills" in the United States "except at lumber centers with a large amount of manufacturing."[5] The new mills became dominant in Blount County during the 1880s, at the same time that frame-house construction was expanding rapidly. The circular saw was invented in England in the eighteenth century and introduced into the United States in the early part of the nineteenth century, but it did not make a great impact until its design was greatly improved in the middle of the nineteenth century.[6] Use of steam power to turn the circular saw began early in the nineteenth century, but at first was confined to stationary sawing activities. Since the steam-powered circular sawmill could saw a log much faster than the water-powered sash sawmill, development of the portable steam-powered circular sawmill had a great impact on rural areas of East Tennessee.

J. Richards, writing in 1872, described a typical portable steam-powered sawmill:

> The circular sawmill of Lane and Bodley [a popular Cincinnati model] . . . is a fair sample of this peculiar mill. The framing in which the machinery is mounted is of iron; the carriage rails and supporting sills are of wood. No foundation is needed beyond a few cross ties. The engine for driving the mill is mounted on trucks, and the whole is strictly portable . . . The feed and supply pumps, shafts, pillow blocks, and all parts of the engine are mounted on the boiler, which is multiflued and has a rectangular fire box large enough to receive slab wood four feet long. The exhaust is carried into the smoke stack, creating a sufficient draught to burn the sawdust which forms the greater share of the fuel.[7]

Blount County newspapers occasionally carried notices of sawmill sales in the latter part of the nineteenth century. The following advertisement, which appeared in *The (Maryville) Republican* on 30 May 1874, provides a description of a portable steam-powered circular sawmill, probably typical of those operating in the county at that time:

> ### FOR SALE
> A first-class steam saw mill, located on Baker's Creek, one mile from Brick Mill, Blount County, Tenn. Said Mill has 54 & 30 inch circular saws, 25 horse power portable engine and boiler, all in good order; the best head blocks in this part of the State. This mill, with 4 hands, is capable of cutting 4000 to 7000 feet of lumber per day. Cause of selling, poor health.[8]

The two saws mentioned in the advertisement were common for portable circular sawmills. One disadvantage of early circular mills was that they could only cut through logs whose diameter was half the diameter of the circular saw. A feature of portable sawmills, however, was the simultaneous use of two circular saws, one above the other, cutting in the same kerf. The use of two saws greatly increased the size of logs that could be sawed.

The great advantage of the portable sawmill was that it was transported to the site of the timber to be cut, rather than the timber being transferred to the mill for sawing. The first portable sawmill in Blount County may have been owned by Jesse Kerr Jr., of Louisville. Kerr purchased a sawmill in 1858 and wrote about its performance shortly after buying the mill:

> I set it up on a small stream that afforded constant water about as thick as my little finger, which was much more than sufficient to supply the boiler. We are able to cut 3,000 feet of beautiful lumber in 12 hours, with something less than one cord of wood. It is the very thing we have so much needed in our country for a long time. With a little trouble and expense, we are able to move it from five to ten miles per day, and set it up in the heart of the timbers, which saves the great burden of hauling the logs a long distance to the mill.[9]

The steam-powered portable sawmill probably arrived in East Tennessee during the early 1850s, although stationary steam-powered mills likely appeared earlier.[10] Advertisements for circular sawmills and portable steam engines appeared in Knoxville newspapers in the early 1850s, and as early as December 1854, the Knoxville Iron Company was manufacturing stationary and portable steam engines and circular sawmills.[11] Advertisements for portable sawmills continued to appear in local newspapers until at least the turn of the century.

A few portable sawmills were operating in East Tennessee during the 1850s, but they were not common until after the Civil War. The number of such mills increased during the 1870s, but not rapidly until the 1880s. In 1874, Killebrew stated that there were three steam sawmills in Blount County, "cutting in the aggregate, from fifteen to twenty thousand feet per day."[12] There is no proof that the three mills were portable units, but they are believed to have been.

The Tenth U.S. Census (1880) listed four steam sawmills for

Blount County, and at least three of them were the portable type. One of the questions that the census taker asked sawmill operators was: "Do you do your own logging?" The answer was "No" for all the water-powered mills, but three of the four steam mill operators replied "Yes" to the question. The fourth operator did not answer the question. That the steam sawmill operators stated that they did their own logging simply means that they were transporting portable sawmills to the site of the timber to be cut.[13]

There is other evidence that the three steam sawmills were of the portable type. The Elkanah Johnson mill, headquartered on the Johnson farm at Alynwick a few miles southwest of Maryville, burned in late May 1879, in the Cloyd's Creek area, along the Blount-Loudon county line near Greenback, several miles from Alynwick.[14] The Robert McClanahan mill, with a home site near Rockford, was reported to be cutting timber in Sevier County in 1904.[15] Older residents of the Louisville area agree that the James Henry mill, headquartered in the Holston College area west of Louisville, was a portable one. According to Ethel Cox Smith, the Henry mill was brought to her grandfather's farm about 1871 to saw timber to build the house in which she now resides.[16] J. E. Prater, born in 1881, recalls the Henry sawmill being brought to the property of his father, "Buffalo" Jim Prater, to cut stands of pine and chestnut in the late 1880s.[17]

Additional evidence of portable sawmill activity has been gathered for the 1870s. For example, Mrs. W.O. Laffell, granddaughter of M.B. Warren, who built the house in which she now resides near Louisville, stated that a sawmill was brought to the Warren farm to saw planks for the construction of the Warren house during 1874–77.[18] The time of construction of the Warren house is confirmed in an 1878 newspaper article, in which M.B. Warren was reported to have recently completed "a most neat and convenient dwelling house" containing fourteen rooms.[19] The sawmill used to cut timber on the Warren farm may have been the James Henry mill mentioned above or the H.G. Mead steam mill, reported destroyed by fire near Holston College in July 1878.[20]

During the 1880s, the number of portable sawmills multiplied in the county. A sample of Blount County newspapers during the decade reveals the presence of at least twenty-three portable mills, and a considerably larger number is believed to have been present. Portable sawmills were so common by the end of the decade that a Maryville newspaper editor declared them to be "fashionable."[21] During 1890–97, the number of portable mills increased to at least thirty-four.[22]

Newspaper accounts gave proof of the portability of the mills during the 1880s and 1890s. The *Maryville Times* of 17 March 1886 reported that "J.G. Newbert passed through town Monday with a portable engine and saw mill from Madisonville, enroute to Ellejoy, where it will be put into operation."[23] In March 1886, the Ellejoy correspondent of the same paper reported that "Keener Bros. will move their steam saw mill from this part in a few days." In April of the same year, the Union Grove correspondent wrote, "Bill Curtis will move his saw mill to this place in a few days."[24] In early 1894, it was reported that James Baker had moved "his saw mill from Sawyer's Creek to Cheoah," and in early 1896 D.W. Trotter's sawmill was moved to saw lumber for Crof Davis.[25] The portable steam engines of the period in essence were steam wagons with four wheels, usually pulled by teams of oxen.[26]

The period of great increase in number and activity of portable sawmills parallels the rise of frame construction in Blount County. In addition to the Cox and Warren houses previously mentioned, there are several other examples of sawmills being brought to farms to saw lumber for use in construction of houses or barns. In 1888, Hugh Gamble of Ellejoy built a two-story frame house with lumber cut from his farm woods by a portable sawmill.[27] In 1890, a portable sawmill was brought to the farm of Samuel L. Pickens near Shooks Gap to cut timber, some of which was dried and used to erect the two-story frame house now owned by his daughter, Bessie Pickens Garrison.[28]

The best evidence of the impact of portable sawmills on housebuilding was discovered for mountainous Cades Cove, where few frame houses were constructed before the turn of the century. Although water-powered sawmills had been in operation in the cove for years, it was not until the portable sawmills arrived in Cades Cove that large numbers of frame houses were built.[29] Portable sawmill activity and frame house building were brisk during spring and summer 1904 in Cades Cove. In May and June of that year, at least four portable sawmills were in operation in the cove, including those owned by Beecher and Post; by John McGill, who in early June "had his sawmill in the Cove for two weeks"; and by S.L. Sparks, who in early June was sawing on Laurel Creek.[30] In early June 1904, the *Maryville Record* indicated that there was a building boom in Cades Cove, reporting that "Cove people go right on building houses" and that George Myers, W.M. Feezell, and J.T. Sparks had finished construction of their residences.[31] The impact of the building surge extended outside Cades Cove, because in June 1904 Ellejoy carpenters W.J. Patty and J.W. Braden purchased "a new outfit of carpenter tools and machinery and are doing carpenter work in Cades Cove."[32]

Available evidence suggests that much of the frame-house building in Blount County during the latter part of the nineteenth century was associated with the advent and diffusion of the portable circular sawmill. In more isolated areas, such as Cades Cove, there appears to have been an even stronger relationship between the appearance of portable sawmills and the construction of frame houses. From the late 1850s until the late 1870s, portable sawmills in the county were used primarily for custom sawing, particularly for relatively affluent residents. The rapid increase in number of sawmills in the 1880s, however, was related to the rise of commercial lumbering, which also played an important role in the rise of frame house construction and the decline of log construction in the county.

The Impact of Commercial Lumbering

Commercial lumbering in Blount County increased significantly during the 1880s and 1890s, in response to a growing local market and northern demand for lumber.[33] The development of commercial lumbering was made possible by post–Civil War railroad construction, which connected Blount County with Knoxville and remote markets.[34] Construction of the Knoxville and Charleston Railroad from Knoxville to Maryville in 1868 was a precursor to the rise of commercial lumbering in Blount County.[35] By the early 1880s, considerable activity was oriented to the railroad, with principal shipping points located at Maryville and Rockford. Maryville, although much larger, lagged behind Rockford as a shipping center for lumber because Rockford had the advantage of being located on both the railroad line and the Little River. Large numbers of logs were floated down the Little River from Tuckaleechee Cove to sawmills at Rockford during the 1880s and 1890s.[36] Much of the activity along the Little River was carried out by northern companies that shipped large amounts of yellow poplar to the East and Midwest.[37] In other parts of the county, lumber was sawed at mills, particularly portable mills, and transported on horse-drawn wagons to Rockford and Maryville for shipment by rail to Knoxville.

Newspapers of the 1880s provide evidence of the increased role of commercial lumbering in the county during that decade. In April 1882, for example, M.B. Gaddis advertised in a Maryville newspaper seeking sixteen teams for hauling logs and lumber.[38] In June of the same year, it was reported that the lumber business was "on the increase" in the county, and during the same month, the Tennessee Lumber Company built a steam sawmill in Tuckaleechee Cove and erected a three-mile-long tramway "in preparation for an extensive lumber business."[39]

In early 1883, a Maryville newspaper mentioned that "the lumber interests of our county seem to be flourishing," and later in the year, two other Blount County newspapers reported that Maryville was undergoing a building boom.[40] By 1886, several lumberyards had been established and much lumber was being shipped out of the county. *The Maryville Times*, in early 1886, reported that R.A. McClanahan in Rockford was "running the lumber business for all it is worth."[41]

An examination of activity in the Ellejoy area in the northeastern section of the county indicates the extent to which timber enterprises and portable sawmills increased in Blount County. Some of this business was in the form of custom work, but much of it was also commercial lumbering.[42] By April 1886, ten different lumber companies were cutting lumber along Ellejoy Creek.[43] Activity such as that near Ellejoy may have been common in other parts of the county as well. For example, the area along the Tennessee River west of Louisville was reported to be saturated with portable sawmills in the late 1880s and early 1890s.[44]

Lumber enterprises were more active in the 1890s than in the previous decade. The floating of logs down the Little River from Tuckaleechee Cove to Rockford, accomplished through the use of "splash dams," received attention in local newspapers. In March 1896, the *Maryville Times* reported that the "Little River got on a boom last week, and the Lumber Company turned a splash loose sending over a thousand logs through the cove."[45] In May 1896, the same newspaper stated, "The Little River Lumber Co. are [sic] continually 'splashing,' and every splash robs old Smoky of some of her valuable timber."[46]

In addition to the exportation of lumber from the county, there was considerable local demand for lumber during the 1890s. Much of that demand was in Maryville, the county seat, where building contractors, sash and blind factories, cabinet and furniture shops, and coffin makers all required lumber to manufacture their products. Some lumbermen specialized in supplying these local manufacturers. One of these, James Thomas of Dry Branch, in the northeastern part of the county, was reported to be furnishing Maryville with "lathes and lumber" in early 1891.[47]

Much of the increased activity of the lumber industry in the 1890s was associated with the construction of the Knoxville Southern Railway through the western part of the county in

1890.[48] The railroad ran parallel to the Tennessee River and passed through the villages of Louisville, Friendsville, Meadow, and Greenback (the latter in Loudon County). As soon as the railroad was completed, shipments of lumber began to be exported from the county. For example, James Bales and Company shipped several carloads of lumber from Friendsville during a one-week period in January 1891.[49] In April of the same year, it was reported that "Jeff Jackson and others are busy hauling lumber from Big Springs [to Friendsville] to ship to Knoxville."[50] Several portable sawmill operators transfered their mills to sites along the railroad to reduce costs of transporting lumber. In May 1892, Cal Davis was preparing to move his mill from Pea Ridge to "down on the Knoxville Southern Railroad," and in October of that year, W.G. Whitney of Block House was in the Cliff community "looking after a point to locate his large saw mill."[51]

The increase in demand for lumber also presented the farmer with a cash crop. When a portable mill came to a farm to saw timber needed to build a house, the cost of sawing was paid with additional timber, which, when sawed, was stacked on wagons and hauled to market. The farmer often sold enough timber not only to pay for his building lumber, but also to have enough money left over to pay for other building materials such as nails, windows, and doors, as well as the labor required to erect the residence.

The extent to which commercial lumbering was related to frame house construction can be seen clearly in the more isolated mountainous areas in southern Blount County. In Cades Cove, for example, few frame residences had been erected before portable sawmills were brought to the area just after the turn of the century. The arrival of portable mills in the mountains was associated with the development of the Little River Lumber Company, founded in 1901 and headquartered at Townsend.[52]

In 1900 the Little River Lumber Company quickly connected the mountains with outside markets by building a railroad which joined Townsend with the Knoxville and Augusta Railroad at

Maryville.[53] Railroads soon were constructed along streams farther into the mountains, where the Little River Lumber Company had purchased 100,000 acres of timberland.[54] Cades Cove native Howard Sparks, born in 1892, remembers the impact of the Little River Lumber Company operations: "Two or three steam portable sawmills were moved into the cove after Little River Railroad came to Townsend about 1902. The wagon haul was shortened now, with most lumber out of the cove delivered to the train depot at Riverside [now Walland] at the lower end of Tuckaleechee Cove."[55] With the construction of the railroad and the arrival of portable sawmills, farmers in Cades Cove were able to have lumber sawed for their construction needs, as well as to sell timber as a cash crop.

Logging and lumbering not only brought a demand for farmers' timber, but also presented an opportunity for Blount residents to become entrepreneurs or workers in the lumber industry. A few Cades Cove farmers established sawmills and some yeomen farmers worked part-time in lumber operations. Sawmill jobs were especially attractive to residents of the Chestnut Flats area of Cades Cove, and such employment made it possible for "tenants on marginal or peripheral land . . . to provide the basic necessities for their families through hard work."[56] Farmers Perry Boyd and Asbury Reed of the Big Springs section of the county worked as members of Yank Neubert's portable sawmill crew during the 1890s and early 1900s.[57] In adjacent Sevier County, steam-engine owners often were farmers who seasonally used their equipment to power both sawmills and wheat-threshing machines.[58] The lumber industry may have provided jobs for a few hundred workers during at least part of the year, and wages earned from such employment contributed to the farmers' ability to construct frame houses.

CHAPTER EIGHT

Innovations in Construction Techniques and the Decline in Log House Building

Changes in sawmilling and the rise of commercial lumbering were active factors that brought about the rapid rise of frame construction and the decline of log construction. The rise in frame construction, however, would have been more difficult without innovations in building construction. Before the Civil War, Blount County houses were of timber frame construction, which required the efforts of a skilled carpenter and helpers and usually took relatively long periods of time to complete. After the Civil War, two lighter construction techniques, balloon framing and box construction, became the accepted modes of house building. Both of these techniques required much less in the way of carpentry skills than did timber frame construction.

The Role of Balloon Construction

After the Civil War, light or "balloon" frame construction spread to East Tennessee and Blount County. Whereas heavy frame construction was based on support of a structure by braced corner posts, balloon construction called for a building to be supported by a series of light posts and studs, all of which equally held up the weight of the structure (fig. 25). Although there are several permutations, balloon framing of the nineteenth century is essentially the same as modern "two-by-four" construction.

The advantages of balloon framing were being propounded for several years before the technique gained acceptance in East Tennessee. Solon Robinson, in 1855, offered a rationale for use of the balloon frame:[1]

> To lay out and frame a building so that all its parts will come together, requires the skill of a master mechanic, and a host of men and a deal of hard work to lift the great sticks of timber into position. To erect a balloon-building requires about as much mechanical skill as it does to build a board fence. Any farmer who is handy with the saw, iron square and hammer, with one of his boys or a common laborer to assist him, can go to work and put up a frame for an outbuilding, and finish it off with his own labor, just as well as to hire a carpenter to score and hew great oak sticks and fill them full of mortices, all by the science of the "square rule." It is a waste of labor that we should all lend our aid to put a stop to. Besides it will enable many a farmer to improve his place with new buildings, who, though he has long needed them, has shuddered at the thought of cutting down half of the best trees in his woodlot, and then giving half a year's work to hauling it home and paying for what I do know is the wholly useless labor of framing.

Balloon construction was developed in Chicago in the early 1830s, as a means of rapidly erecting inexpensive buildings during the city's tremendous growth.[2] This light construction technique quickly spread through the Midwest and subsequently to the West, where it was instrumental in the development and expansion of cities and particularly in San Francisco's growth during the Gold Rush days.[3] Although the new construction method eventually was accepted throughout the country, it may not have penetrated the South until after the Civil War. According to Patrick, joinery was replaced by the nailed balloon frame in Tennessee about 1870.[4]

Fig. 25. Balloon-frame construction in Knox County (1986).

To assess the rate of acceptance of balloon construction in Blount County, it is important to know the balloon technique prescribed before the Civil War. Robinson offered the following as the proper method of balloon construction in 1855:

> a great many farmers would like to know how to build a farmhouse for half the present expense. I therefore ask the indulgence of the Club, while I start a balloon from the foundation, and finish it . . . I would saw all my timber for a frame-house, or ordinary frame outbuilding, of the following dimensions: Two inches by eight; two by four; two by one . . . First, level your foundation, and lay down two of the two by eight pieces, flatwise, for sidewalls. Upon these set the floor-sleeps, on edge, thirty-two inches apart. Fasten one at each end, and perhaps, one or two in the middle, if the building is large, with a wooden pin. These end-sleepers are the end-sills. Now lay the floor . . . It is a great saving . . . of labor, to begin at the bottom of a house

and build up. In laying the floor first, you have no studs to cut and fit around, and can let your boards run out over the ends, just as it happens, and afterwards saw them off smooth by the sill. Now set up a corner-post, which is nothing but one of the two-by-four studs, fastening the bottom by four nails; make it plumb, and stay it each way. Set another at the other corner, and then mark off your door and window places, and set up the side-studs and put in the frames. Fill up with studs between, sixteen inches apart, supporting the top by a line or strip of board from corner to corner, or stayed studs between. Now cover that side with rough sheeting boards, unless you intend to side-up with clap-boards on the studs, which I never would do, except for a small, common building. Make no calculation about the top of the studs; wait until you get up that high. You may use them of any length, with broken or stud-shot ends, no matter. When you have got this side boarded as high as you can reach, proceed to set up another. In the meantime, other workmen can be lathing the first side. When you have got the sides all up, fix upon the height of your upper floor, and strike a line upon the studs for the under side of the joist. Cut out a joist four inches wide, half-inch deep, and nail on firmly one of the inch strips. Upon these strips rest the chamber floor joist. Cut out a joist one inch deep, in the lower edge, and lock it on the strip, and nail each joist to each stud. Now lay this floor, and go on to build the upper story, as you did the lower one; splicing on and lengthening out studs or wherever needed, until you get high enough for the plate. Splice studs or joist by simply butting the end together, and nailing strips on each side. Strike a line and saw off the top of the studs even upon each side—not the ends—and nail on one of the inch strips. That is the plate. Cut the ends of the upper joist the bevel of the pitch of the roof, and nail them fast to the plate, placing the end one inside the studs, which you will let run promiscuously, to be cut off by the rafter. Now lay the garret-floor by all means before you put on the roof, and you will find that you have saved fifty percent of hard labor.[5]

The period from the end of the Civil War to around 1890 was one of transition from heavy- to light-frame construction in Blount County. The Dr. Andrew Jackson Taylor house, built in the northeastern part of the county in 1868–69, used construction methods similar to the light or balloon techniques prescribed by Robinson in 1855. Conversely, the Elisha Jones house, built near Friendsville in 1884, was of braced and joined timber frame construction. Other such "light" and "heavy" frame houses were built during the period. Most represented a shift toward balloon construction, although most structures had elements heavier than those recommended by Robinson.

By the mid-1880s, most houses being built in the county could be called balloon, having been erected with lighter materials than previously and held together completely with nails. In the 1880s, residences were constructed in Maryville and other towns and villages much as Robinson had suggested. Country farmhouses, however, generally were of somewhat heavier materials, especially the sills, floor sleepers, and corner posts. In the 1890s, house construction in the county was typically lighter than in the 1880s, and most houses could be described as balloon structures, although some employed an even lighter innovation, box construction.

Balloon dwellings could be erected much more cheaply, quickly, and simply than timber frame houses, and the use of the balloon frame coincided with the rise of frame construction and the decline of log construction in Blount County. The acceptance of the balloon frame made possible the rapid construction of houses and other buildings in Maryville and smaller settlements in the 1880s and 1890s. The same is true for rural areas, where many farmers would have erected log residences, had not the balloon frame been known and accepted.

The Role of Box Construction

In addition to balloon framing, another building innovation, "box" construction, contributed greatly to the decline of log construc-

Fig. 26. Board-and-batten box house, constructed c. 1900 (1988).

tion in Blount County. Box construction, consisting of a single wall of vertical planks rather than the conventional double-wall technique, was much easier and cheaper to build than balloon framing (fig. 26). In typical box construction, "sills are placed on a foundation, wide boards are nailed on vertically at each corner, and a two-by-four [wall plate] is nailed on horizontally along the tops of these vertical boards . . . Additional vertical boards are attached to form a single-thickness wall . . . narrow strips of wood are nailed on outside over the cracks to produce board-and-batten siding."[6] A few Blount County houses were supported by two-by-four corner posts as well as studs to support windows and doors.

Although vertical plank wall construction developed relatively recently in East Tennessee, its existence in New England dates to the seventeenth century.[7] Plank wall construction is believed to have evolved from grooved-post construction which was brought to the New World from Europe, probably from Scandinavia.[8] Vertical plank construction did not, however, become very popular in the United States, where the timber frame and subsequent balloon frame generally were sided with horizontal clapboards.

Vertical board-and-batten siding as a frame covering was popularized in the books of several American architects from the late 1830s through the 1850s.[9] Board-and-batten may have enjoyed some popularity in parts of the country before the Civil War, but no evidence of its acceptance in antebellum East Tennessee has been uncovered. Some years after the Civil War, however, the board-and-batten box house became popular in the South,[10] and by the turn of the century it was the "prevailing house type" in Appalachia.[11] It is not known when box construction first appeared in East Tennessee, but a few such houses may have been built in Blount County during the late 1870s. Box houses became common in the county during the 1880s, and larger numbers were erected during the 1890s and early 1900s. Relatively few of the pre-1900 box houses, perhaps fifty, remained visible in the county's landscape in an unmodified form at the time of writing.

Because the board-and-batten box houses were not built as well as the heavier, weatherboarded balloon houses, a higher percentage of the box structures had been abandoned or destroyed by the early 1980s. By contrast, many of Blount County's original box houses still existed, but in different forms. Often they had had their battens stripped off and replaced with conventional horizontal siding, although some of them were sided with weatherboarding at the time of their original construction. In addition, a number of box houses had been converted to balloon-frame structures, with the insertion of corner posts and wall studs and an inside wall. Finally, some box houses had been camouflaged by the addition of modern siding such as asbestos shingle, aluminum siding, and vinyl siding.

Although some yeomen farmers built box houses, most of these houses were associated with relatively poor people, and a large number were constructed as tenant houses.[12] According to J.E. Prater, his father, "Buffalo" Jim Prater, built two box houses for tenants on his Tennessee River farm in the late 1880s.[13] Two box houses, erected by Dr. Sam Lane for his tenants in the 1880s or 1890s, remain on the old Lane farm in the Brick Mill community.[14] At the turn of the century, in neighboring Sevier County many small farmers and townfolk had "houses with only single board walls . . . boards were up and down, nailed at the top and bottom with no studs."[15]

Box construction played an important role in the decline of log construction during the latter part of the nineteenth century. Board-and-batten houses were built for both economic and social reasons. They required much less material to construct than did balloon or log buildings, and they required little skill or time to erect. Two or three men easily could erect a box house, whereas six or eight men were needed to raise a log house.[16] A landlord was attracted to a "boxed" tenant house primarily because of its low cost. Without the knowledge and acceptance of box construction, landlords often would have selected log construction over balloon framing. From the tenant's perspective, a new box house, plain as it was, probably was an attractive perquisite of tenancy with a particular landlord.

The small farmer undoubtedly was impressed by the low cost of construction of the box house. Perhaps as importantly, however, the box house represented a chance for a poor farmer to discard his log house and live in a more socially acceptable sawn plank house. Without the possibility of building a box residence, the poor farmer likely would have built a log house rather than the more expensive balloon frame house. A.E. Scott, visiting the western North Carolina mountains in 1884, indicated that the box house had a higher status in the area than a log dwelling:

> We soon arrived at his brother's house—a house made of sawed lumber, and more pretentious than the log cabins of the region. The cracks between the rough boards were even battened, and it had several openings intended eventually for glass windows. The usual broad veranda stretched across the front, and huge

stone chimneys stood outside each end. Inside it was divided by a board partition into two rooms, and each room had outside doors opening front and back.[17]

The decision by a small farmer to build a flimsy box house in place of a log structure was not necessarily a wise one. Ella Enslow offered a low opinion of box houses when compared with the log houses of the Appalachian hollow in which she lived in the early part of the century: "That single inch-thick skin of plank with leaking crevices is a far poorer protection against cold than log walls, which can make a room very snug in winter."[18] According to Charles E. Martin, a box-house wall "had only about one-fifth the insulation capability of a hewn log wall."[19]

In spite of the obvious inadequacies of box house construction, the board-and-batten plank dwelling became popular in Blount County during the late nineteenth century. The building's cheapness of construction made it possible for the members of the poorer class to discard their log houses and live in residences that they believed enhanced their social status. If the acceptance of balloon construction accelerated the decline in log house construction, the increased popularity of box construction near the turn of the century signaled log construction's ultimate demise.

The role of the box house may have been greater in Blount County than has been recognized, because there likely were more weatherboarded box houses in the county than in the buildings survey identified. It is often difficult to identify these more substantial box houses, which were built with a double-layer single wall (horizontal boards over vertical boards); a few such structures probably were labeled as balloon-frame houses. Other structures, originally of double-box construction and correctly identified as "double-box" houses, may have been surveyed incorrectly as houses modified from single-layer to double-layer construction through the addition of weatherboarding. Surveys done in the late 1980s in Hawkins and Johnson counties, in upper East Tennessee, revealed the existence of several box houses originally built with double-layer walls, and some of the box houses in Arkansas also exhibit weatherboard siding.[20]

We may conclude, then, that the decline of log house construction and concomitant rise of frame house construction likely would have been delayed had it not been for innovations in light construction techniques. After the Civil War, balloon framing spread to East Tennessee, and by the mid-1880s, the balloon frame had replaced the timber frame in house building in Blount County. The advantages of balloon frame construction were that buildings could be erected quickly and relatively cheaply and that such construction required minimal carpentry skills. The introduction of box construction, even cheaper and easier to build than balloon framing, probably was the factor most responsible for the virtual demise of log construction during the 1890s.

CHAPTER NINE

Conclusion

During the course of our field work, gathering background information on log house form and construction characteristics, it became evident that some conclusions in the literature about Upland South and Tennesse log houses are inaccurate when applied to East Tennessee. East Tennessee log houses do not fit neatly into the rectangular/square-pen dichotomy put forth by Glassie and subsequently stressed by Jordan. A significant number of East Tennessee structures surveyed were either oblong pens, with dimensions intermediate between the dimensions prescribed for rectangular and square houses, or square pens that were larger than expected. East Tennessee log pens may provide evidence that the ethnic associations of pen form had become blurred by the time log construction spread to the area. The typical double-pen log house in East Tennessee was not the dogtrot type reported by Scofield and Crutchfield to be dominant in the state of Tennessee. All three double-pen house types proved common in East Tennessee, but field data indicated that the saddlebag house was the most numerous type.

The view that cultural tradition accounts for geographical patterns of corner notches on log houses has been challenged by scholars who claim that timber type is a predictor of notch type. However, on the East Tennessee log houses surveyed, notches exhibited little association with timber type and appeared to be the product of cultural tradition and not an adaptation to an environmental condition.

Several reasons have been presented in the literature for the decline of log house construction, but in the study area, only changes in sawmilling and lumbering and innovations in construction techniques were found to have played major roles in the decline of log construction. The changing agricultural economy appears to have been of little importance, and it is difficult to assess the influence of wealth and social stigma, although both were responsible for the abandonment of some log houses as well as the construction of some frame structures in Blount County.

A significant discovery is the strong correlation between the decline of log construction and rise of light or balloon framing and even lighter box construction. No such relationship has been established previously in the literature, although both Wilson and Hutslar appear to imply the existence of a relationship between the decline in log construction and the rise of balloon framing, and Eller and Tebbetts have stressed the importance of the box house as a landscape element in Appalachia and Arkansas. Balloon-frame and box construction both were firmly established throughout the South during the latter half of the nineteenth century, and it seems highly likely that, in other areas of post–Civil War log construction, both construction techniques played a role similar to that in Blount County. Moreover, if log house construction declined rapidly in a particular area, it would have been virtually impossible for the antecedent heavy timber frame house— which required considerable time, effort, and carpentry skills to construct—to have replaced rapidly the log dwelling.

The role that balloon framing played in providing the housing urgently needed in upstart American towns has been recognized by Boorstin, but little is known of the actual pattern of diffusion of balloon construction.[1] Was there, for example, a hierarchical diffusion of the balloon-frame house, from large cities to smaller cities and eventually to small towns? If so, did rural areas around larger cities and towns receive and accept it before other rural areas? If that was the case, the decline of log construction should have been slower in rural areas around small settlements than in areas which first accepted the balloon frame.

Even less is known about the history of box construction than about that of balloon construction in the United States. Box houses often are observed in photos of early mining and timber settlements of the Upland South. Was the spread of such settlements responsible for the early diffusion of the box house in the South, or were such mining settlements the recipients of a spreading construction innovation?

The decline in log construction in Blount County is associated with an increase in the number of sawmills, the advent of portable steam-powered circular sawmills, and the rise of commercial lumbering. The increase in number of sawmills has been mentioned as a factor critical in the decline of log construction by Eller for Appalachia and by Zelinsky for Georgia. It is difficult, however, to imagine the rapid decline of log construction in most parts of the Upland South without the portable sawmill, because lumbering operations then would have been limited only to stream sites. Extending Zelinsky's work would likely reveal that many of the sawmills he reported being added in Georgia after the Civil War were, in fact, portable mills. The literature has established that some of the neighborhood mills of Appalachia, cited by Eller as important in the decline of log construction, also were portable mills.

During the late 1890s and early 1900s, there were as many as forty steam-powered portable circular sawmills in the Tellico Plains area of East Tennessee, forming part of the initial thrust of commercial lumbering into that part of the region.[2] It would be logical to expect that the shift from log to frame construction in the Tellico Plains area would have coincided with the spread of the portable sawmill. Because the portable mills were cutting "the smaller timber of farmers and residents of the Tellico area," some of those selling timber most likely retained lumber to build a house and also used money derived from the sale of timber to pay for construction costs of the house.[3]

There was a strong correlation between the diffusion of the portable sawmill and the rise of commercial lumbering in Blount County. Commercial lumbering provided local lumber supplies but also prepared lumber for export from the county. The rise of commercial lumbering was greatly facilitated by the construction of railroads, which opened regional and distant markets for Blount County lumber. At the same time, railroads served to bring goods into Blount County from outside areas. Imported goods might have included lumber for purchase, but there is no evidence that Blount County relied on imported lumber during the nineteenth century. If log-house dwellers had had access to imported lumber and could afford to buy it, they could have built frame houses without the presence of local sawmills. No evidence, of such occurrences, however, has been discovered for Blount County.

Further research should be carried out in an area of the Upland South where log houses were dominant at the time of railroad construction and where there were little or no local commercial logging and sawing operations. The purpose of such research would be to determine if railroad penetration alone resulted in the decline of log construction in a particular area. Willis has stated that, in southwestern Virginia, log construction declined as railroads, coal mining, and timber operations came to the area. Were there areas where railroads penetrated and coal mining developed but commercial logging and sawmilling did not develop? If so, did log construction decline without the presence of local timber activities?

Pillsbury and Hutslar have indicated that the persistence and decline of log construction in Pennsylvania and Ohio were related to the degree of affluence in a particular area. That is, log construction declined first in affluent areas and remained longest in poor areas. In Blount County, wealth was associated with antebellum non-log house construction because brick- and frame-house builders were affluent farmers and merchants. However, such a relationship is difficult to establish for the postbellum period, in which log houses were replaced by frame or box structures. In fact, by 1890 either frame or box construction was associated with virtually all segments of the rural community. Increased wealth derived from the sale of farm timber made frame houses possible for some residents of the county, but there is a lack of documentation of a general relationship between wealth and house construction during the late 1800s in Blount County.

Pillsbury and Hutslar may have been correct in their assessment of reasons for the persistence and decline of log construction in Pennsylvania and Ohio. Their conclusions cannot be accepted, however, until evidence of historic and regional patterns of log house construction decline is presented and then compared with patterns of affluence. According to Hutslar, log house construction had declined in most areas of Ohio by 1850, and although Pillsbury provides no evidence, it is likely that the same was true of Pennsylvania. If log house construction did decline before 1850 in those areas, and if the decline was related to wealth, it could be hypothesized that, in other areas where log construction lasted for longer periods—especially areas pervaded by the log house during the post–Civil War period—the decline of log dwelling construction was not strongly related to significant increases in wealth. Other factors, such as access to sawmills and lumber and innovations in light construction techniques, made it considerably cheaper to build a frame house than before the Civil War, and this cost factor was a crucial incentive to change.

There is evidence that Cades Cove, in Blount County, was richer than many other sections of the county at the beginning of the twentieth century. The people of Cades Cove, however, still were living in log houses, while those in some sections of the county had, for the most part, built frame or box houses. It was a lack of access to sawmills, especially portable sawmills, and to lumber that made Cades Cove perhaps the last area in Blount County to have most of its families still living in log houses.

Lounsbury has associated the decline of self-sufficient building techniques, in which he included log construction, in North

Carolina with the rise of a market-oriented agricultural economy. No evidence has been uncovered to document such a relationship in Blount County during the late 1800s, although the construction of railroads during that period offered farmers greater access to markets than had existed during earlier periods.

One of the problems in comparing Blount County findings with those of Lounsbury for North Carolina is that he implied that log construction had declined during the antebellum period. That implication is not completely accurate, since there is little doubt that the log house was the dominant dwelling in much of mountainous western North Carolina during the late 1800s. It is also unlikely that most of western North Carolina had shifted from a self-sufficient agricultural economy to a highly commercial agricultural economy by that time. Lounsbury apparently generalizes about the whole state of North Carolina based on findings from the more agriculturally oriented coastal plain and piedmont sections of the state. Although further research is needed before "a changing agricultural economy" can be fully evaluated as a factor in bringing about the demise of log construction, investigation of the topic will be made difficult for some areas because U.S. census manuscripts are missing for 1890.

Jordan suggested that the social stigma of living in a log house contributed greatly to the decline in construction of such buildings in nineteenth-century Texas, and Wilson stated that change from a log to a frame house represented a step toward a higher social status in Alabama. It is likely that by the latter part of the nineteenth century, many East Tennesseans also considered it socially unacceptable to live in nonsided log houses, but little evidence of a social stigma has been documented for Blount County. To be sure, the widespread acceptance of the box house during the late 1800s may indicate that at least some Blount Countians preferred to live in frame houses of the poorest quality rather than in more substantial log houses.

Evidence of variations in the period of decline of log house construction, within relatively small areas, may indicate that social stigma was of minor importance in bringing about change in type of house construction. For example, the same social pressure to replace log houses with frame ones may have existed in Cades Cove as in certain other parts of Blount County, even though the time of frame construction was later in Cades Cove.

Peirce Lewis has stated that rapid landscape change usually is "provoked by such great events as wars, depressions, and major inventions."[4] In Blount County, it appears that technological innovations (light construction techniques and the portable sawmill), the rise of commercial lumbering, and railroad construction were the major events that, acting in concert, provoked the shift to frame construction.

Additional research is needed to improve our understanding of spatial-temporal patterns of log house dominance and decline, as well as of the factors responsible for the existence of such patterns. An understanding of such patterns can lead to conclusions about the changing character of areas. A decline in log house construction may indicate, for example, that a particular area has become less isolated and is converging culturally with other areas where frame construction is already common.

If one is to understand the reasons for the decline of log house construction in an area, it is imperative that the historical pattern of decline be described accurately. This study has shown that log house construction declined rapidly during the 1880s and 1890s in Blount County. This finding does not represent an unexpected occurrence, but simply illustrates Lewis' concept of landscape change, that of "historic lumpiness." This concept holds that "most major cultural change does not occur gradually, but instead in great sudden historic leaps."

A rapid decline in log construction is consistent with the findings of some students of log construction, but such a shift has not been reported by others who have addressed the subject. Jordan has stated that there was a precipitous decline in log construction in Texas, where it lasted from about 1815 to 1940, with construction of log dwellings lasting approximately thirty to fifty years in eastern Texas, the part of the state where most log structures were built.[6] In constrast, Zelinsky claims that in Georgia, log house construction declined steadily after the Civil War until the 1950s.[7] Others, such as Pillsbury, writing on log construction in Pennsylvania, offer reasons for the decline of log house construction, but provide no information on the time of the decline.[8]

One can conclude that the reasons given in the literature for the decline of log construction not only are assertions, but in some cases are based on imprecise historical data. This work represents the first detailed study of the decline of log house construction, and a subsequent study should use the findings of this work as hypotheses to be tested in another area.

This study has contributed to a better understanding of the pattern and causes of change of a once-dominant landscape element in rural East Tennessee. Research on the changing status of an element of the cultural landscape has additional value because it can demonstrate, as this study has, that a change in the status of a basic landscape element is indicative of other socioeconomic or technological changes. Such studies therefore are important because they contribute to a better understanding of the evolving character of places.

Notes

Chapter One

1. Studies entirely or partially devoted to characteristics of log house construction and their associated geographical and historical patterns in the eastern United States include Henry Glassie, "The Appalachian Log Cabin," *Mountain Life and Work* 39, no. 4 (1963): 5–14; Glassie, "Types of the Southern Mountain Cabin," in *The Study of American Folklore*, ed. Jan H. Brunvand, (New York: Norton, 1968), 338–70; Donald Hutslar, *The Architecture of Migration: Log Construction in the Ohio Country, 1750–1850* (Athens: Ohio Univ. Press, 1986); Terry G. Jordan, *Texas Log Buildings* (Austin: Univ. of Texas Press, 1978), *American Log Buildings* (Chapel Hill: Univ. of North Carolina Press, 1986), and "Log Construction in the East Cross Timbers of Texas," *Proceedings of Pioneer America Society* 2 (1973): 107–124; Terry G. Jordan and Matti Kaups, *The American Backwoods Frontier* (Baltimore: John Hopkins Univ. Press, 1989); Fred Kniffen and Henry Glassie, "Building in Wood in the Eastern United States: A Time-Place Perspective," *Geographical Review* 56 (1966):40–66; William Lynwood Montell and Michael Lynn Morse, *Kentucky Folk Architecture* (Lexington: Univ. Press of Kentucky, 1976); Milton B. Newton, Jr., and Linda Pulliam-DiNapoli, "Log Houses as Public Occasions: A Historical Theory," *Annals of the Association of American Geographers* 67 (1977):360–83; Harold R. Shurtleff, *The Log Cabin Myth* (Gloucester, Mass.: Peter Smith, 1967): C.A. Weslager, *The Log Cabin in America* (New Brunswick, N.J..: Rutgers Univ. Press, 1969); Eugene Wilson, *Alabama Folk Houses* (Montgomery: Alabama Historical Commission, 1975); and Wilbur Zelinsky, "The Log House in Georgia," *Geographical Review*, 43 (1953):173–93.

2. Harriette Simpson Arnow, *Seedtime on the Cumberland* (New York: Macmillan, 1960), 273–74; John Richard Dennett, *The South As It Is: 1865–1866* (New York: Viking, 1965), 95, 166, 185, 243; Glassie, "Appalachian Log Cabin," 10; J.B. Killebrew, *The Resources of Tennessee*

(Nashville: Tavel, Eastman and Howell, 1874), 438, 459, 551–52; Kniffen and Glassie, "Building in Wood," 48–66; Montell and Morse, *Kentucky Folk Architecture*, 9, 16; Robert Somers, *The Southern States Since the War, 1870–71* (University: Univ. of Alabama Press, 1965, reprint of 1871 ed.), 118–19, 275; Weslager, *Log Cabin in America*, 126–32; Stanley Willis, "Log Houses in Southwest Virginia," *Virginia Cavalcade* 21, no. 4 (1972):37.

3. An exception is Glassie, "Southern Mountain Cabin," which examines both frame and log structures and includes several East Tennessee counties as part of the study area.

4. John Fraser Hart, *The Look of the Land* (Englewood Cliffs, N.J.: Prentice-Hall, 1975), 153.

5. Fred B. Kniffen, "Folk Housing: Key to Diffusion," *Annals* 55 (1965): 549.

6. Fred B. Kniffen, "To Know the Land and Its People," *Landscape* 9, no. 3 (1960):22; and Peirce F. Lewis, "Axioms for Reading the Landscape," in *The Interpretation of Ordinary Landscapes*, ed. D.W. Meinig, (New York: Oxford Univ. Press, 1979), 15.

7. Peirce F. Lewis, "Common Houses, Cultural Spoor," *Landscape* 19, no. 2 (1975):3.

8. Jordan, *Texas Log Buildings*, 5; Eugene Wilson, *Alabama Folk Houses*, 73.

9. Carl Lounsbury, "The Building Process in Antebellum North Carolina," *North Carolina Historical Review* 60 (1983):435.

10. Richard Pillsbury, "Patterns in the Folk and Vernacular House Forms of the Pennsylvania Culture Region," *Pioneer America* 9, no. 1 (1977):29.

11. Hutslar, *Architecture of Migration*, 38.

12. Willis, "Log Houses in Southwest Virginia," 37.

13. Ronald D. Eller, *Miners, Millhands, and Mountaineers* (Knoxville: Univ. of Tennessee Press, 1982), 23.

14. Ibid., 26.

15. Zelinsky, "Log House in Georgia," 181.

16. Kniffen and Glassie, "Building in Wood," 42.

17. Hutslar, *Architecture of Migration*, 38.

18. Eugene Wilson, *Alabama Folk Houses*, 25–26.

19. Inez E. Burns, *History of Blount County, Tennessee* (Nashville: Benson Printing Co., 1957), 277.

20. Adele McKenzie, Maryville, Tenn., interview, June 1985; Durwood Dunn, *Cades Cove* (Knoxville: Univ. of Tennessee Press, 1988), 38.

21. "Historic Buildings Survey of Blount County, Tennessee," completed 1984, on file at Tennessee Historical Commission, Nashville.

22. Burns, *Blount County*; A. Randolph Shields, *The Cades Cove Story* (Gatlinburg, Tenn.: Great Smoky Mountains Natural History Association, 1977); Dunn, *Cades Cove*.

Chapter Two

1. Shurtleff, *Log Cabin Myth*. The term "myth" refers to historians' unfounded association of log houses with early-17th-century English settlements, including Jamestown.

2. Ibid., 20–21, 59; and Glassie, "Appalachian Log Cabin," 5. Upon arrival in America, English settlers often built temporary structures and sometimes copied Indian wigwam huts, which were made of vertical poles. The first permanent houses, however, were of half-timber and heavy frame construction, although some brick houses were erected as soon as brick could be imported.

3. Weslager, *Log Cabin in America*, 126–32; quote, 130.

4. Jordan and Kaups, *American Backwoods Frontier*, 137.

5. Ibid., 135–210; Kniffen and Glassie, "Building in Wood," 58–59; Glassie, "Appalachian Log Cabin," 5–6.

6. Terry G. Jordan and Lester Rowntree, *The Human Mosaic: A Thematic Introduction to Cultural Geography* (San Francisco: Canfield Press, 1976), 13.

7. Jordan, *American Log Buildings*, 7.

8. Frederick Jackson Turner, *The Frontier in American History* (New York: Henry Holt, 1920), 164.

9. Jordan and Rowntree, *Human Mosaic*, 12; Wilbur Zelinsky, *The Cultural Geography of the United States* (Englewood Cliffs, N.J.: Prentice-Hall, 1973), 118–19.

10. Milton Newton, "Cultural Preadaptation and the Upland South," *Geoscience and Man* 5 (1974):149. For additional discussion and a map of culture areas in the U.S., see Henry Glassie, *Pattern in the Material Folk Culture of the Eastern United States* (Philadelphia: Univ. of Pennsylvania Press, 1968), 33–158.

11. Jordan, *American Log Buildings*, 146–49; Jordan and Kaups, *American Backwoods Frontier*, 135–208.

12. Terry G. Jordan, "A Reappraisal of Fenno-Scandian Antecedents for Mildand American Log Construction," *Geographical Review*, 73 (1983): 94.

13. Jordan and Kaups, *American Backwoods Frontier*, 209.

14. Jordan, "Reappraisal of Fenno-Scandian Antecedents," 94. The "doctrine of first effective settlement" appears in Zelinsky, *Cultural Geography*, 13.

15. The standard work on the subject of the diffusion of folk housing from eastern culture hearths in Kniffen, "Folk Housing." Other discussions of the spread of Midland folk architecture are found in, e.g., Peirce F. Lewis, "Common Houses"; and Glassie, *Material Folk Culture*, 36–64.

16. Kniffen and Glassie, "Building in Wood," 58–65; Glassie, "Appalachian Log Cabin," 5; and Jordan, *Texas Log Buildings*, 23–26.

17. Kniffen, "Folk Housing," 549–77.

18. Fred B. Kniffen, "On Corner Timbering," *Pioneer America* 1, no. 1 (1969):1.

19. Kniffen and Glassie, "Building in Wood," 58–59; Jordan and Kaups, *American Backwoods Frontier*, 146–47.

20. Ibid., 63; Glassie, "Appalachian Log Cabin," 10–11; Mary Ann Gusler, "Folk Housing in Patrick County, Virginia," (M.A. thesis, Arizona State Univ., 1973), 52–74; Jordan and Kaups, *American Backwoods Frontier*, 151–55.

21. Kniffen and Glassie, "Building in Wood," 63.

22. Ibid.

23. Jordan and Kaups, *American Backwoods Frontier*, 233–36, 247.

24. John Solomon Otto and Nain Estelle Anderson, "The Diffusion of Upland South Folk Culture, 1790–1840," *Southeastern Geographer* 22 (1982):89–98.

25. Jordan and Kaups, *American Backwoods Frontier*, 233–51; quote, 250.

26. Newton, "Cultural Preadaptation," 152–53.

27. Gilbert Imlay, *A Topographical Description of the Western Territory of North America* (London: F. Debrett, 1797, 3d ed.), 166.

28. F.A. Michaux, *Travels to the West of the Allegheny Mountains*

(London: B. Crosby and Co. and J.P. Hughes, 1805); rptd. in Reuben Gold Thwaites, ed., *Early Western Travels, 1748–1846*, v. 3 (Cleveland, Ohio: Arthur Clark, 1904), 105–306; quote, 300.

29. Michaux, *Travels*, 265–66.
30. Ibid., 270.
31. Ibid., 198–99.
32. Ibid., 184, 186.
33. Eastin Morris, *The Tennessee Gazeteer* (Nashville: W. Hasell Hunt and Co., 1834), 59; and James Patrick, *Architecture in Tennessee, 1768–1897* (Knoxville: Univ. of Tennessee Press, 1981), 17.
34. Frederick Law Olmsted, *A Journey in the Back Country* (New York: Burt Franklin, 1970, reprint of 1860 ed.), 196–200, 205, 208, 220, 230–31, 233–37, 244, 257–58, 262, 267, 276–78.
35. Ibid., 205–206.
36. Ibid., 208.
37. Ibid., 230.
38. Henry M. Christman, "Introduction," in Dennett, *The South*, v–xi.
39. Dennett, *The South*, 95.
40. Ibid., 166, 243.
41. Ibid., 185.
42. Somers, *Southern States*, 118–19.
43. Ibid.
44. Ibid., 275.
45. Horace Kephart, *Our Southern Highlanders* (Knoxville: Univ. of Tennessee Press, 1976; reprint of 1922 ed.; orig. pub. 1913), 30–31; William A. Nesbitt, "History of Early Settlement and Land Use on the Bent Creek Experimental Forest, Buncombe, N.C." (report prepared for Appalachian Forest Experiment Station, Asheville, N.C., 1941), p. 67.
46. John C. Campbell, *The Southern Highlander and His Homeland* (Lexington: Univ. Press of Kentucky, 1969; reprint of 1921 ed.), 82–83; Mandel Sherman and Thomas R. Henry, *Hollow Folk* (New York: Thomas Y. Crowell, 1933), 1, 5.

Chapter Three

1. Evidence for the importance of 18th- and 19th-century log buildings in East Tennessee is found in various sources, including James. A. Crutchfield, "Pioneer Architecture in Tennessee," *Tennessee Historical Quarterly* 35 (1976):162–74; Thomas Hughes, *Rugby Tennessee* (London: Macmillan, 1881), 63, 70; Killebrew, *Resources of Tennessee*, 438, 459, 551–52, 773; John Morgan, "An Examination of Log Dwelllings in a Cumberland Plateau County of East Tennessee," in *Proceedings of Conference on Appalachian Geography* (Athens, W.Va.: Geography Dept., Concord College, 1982), 113–25; John Morgan and Joy Medford, "Log Houses in Grainger County, Tennessee," *Tennessee Anthropologist* 5, no. 2 (1980):137–58; John Morgan and Ashby Lynch, Jr., "The Log Barns of Blount County, Tennessee," *Tennessee Anthropologist* 9, no. 2 (1984): 85–103; Patrick, *Architecture in Tennessee*, 16–17; John B. Rehder, John Morgan, and Joy L. Medford, "The Decline of Smokehouses in Grainger County, Tennessee," *West Georgia College Studies in the Social Sciences* 18 (1979):75–83; Edna Scofield, "The Evolution and Development of Tennessee Houses," *Journal of Tennessee Academy of Science* 11 (1936):229–40.

2. Killebrew, *Resources of Tennessee*, 438, 459, 551–52, 557, 773.

3. Tennessee Valley Authority, *Agricultural and Industrial Survey of Grainger County, Tennessee* (Knoxville: Tennessee Valley Authority, 1934); U.S. Dept. of Agriculture, "The Farm Housing Survey," Misc. Publication No. 323, 1939, table 2.

4. The building surveys are on file at the Tennessee Historical Commission, Nashville.

5. Glassie, "Appalachian Log Cabin," 8.

6. Glassie, "Southern Mountain Cabin," 338–70; Jordan, *Texas Log Buildings*, 108–111.

7. Ibid.

8. James R. O'Malley and John B. Rehder, "The Two-Story Log House in the Upland South," *Journal of Popular Culture* 11 (1978):904–15.

9. Jordan and Kaups, *American Backwoods Frontier*, 209.

10. Ibid.; Norbert F. Riedl, Donald B. Ball, and Anthony P. Cavender, *A Survey of Traditional Architecture and Related Material Folk Culture Patterns in the Normandy Reservoir, Coffee County, Tennessee*, (Knoxville: Tennessee Valley Authority, 1976), 79–89.

11. Jordan and Kaups, *American Backwoods Frontier*, 193–96.
12. Scofield, "Tennessee Houses," 232.
13. Crutchfield, "Pioneer Architecture," 173.
14. Kniffen, "Folk Housing," 56; Glassie, *Material Folk Culture*, 88–89; and Richard H. Hulan, "Middle Tennessee and the Dogtrot House," *Pioneer America* 7, no. 2 (1975):37–46.
15. Michael Ann Williams, "Rethinking the House: Interior Space and Social Change," *Appalachian Journal* 14 (1987):174–89.
16. Kniffen, "Folk Housing," 549.
17. James Ross O'Malley, "The 'I' House: An Indicator of Agricultural Attainment in the Southern Appalachian Valley," in *West Virginia and Appalachia*, ed. Howard G. Adkins, Steve Ewing, and Chester E. Zimolzak (Dubuque, Iowa: Kendall-Hunt, 1977) 105–114.
18. For a discussion of notching techniques, see Kniffen, "On Corner Timbering," 1–8; Kniffen and Glassie, "Building in Wood," 48–57; Jordan and Kaups, *American Backwoods Frontier*, 141–62.
19. Fred Kniffen, "Book Review of *Texas Log Buildings* by Jordan," *Annals of the Association of American Geographers* 69 (1979):331.
20. Jordan, *Texas Log Buildings*, 76.
21. Warren E. Roberts, "Folk Architecture in Context: The Folk Museum," *Proceedings of Pioneer America Society* 1 (1972):38.
22. Milton Newton, Jr., and Pulliam-DiNapoli, "Log Houses as Public Occasions," 373.
23. Ibid., 377–79; Kniffen and Glassie, "Building in Wood," 63–64; Morgan and Medford, "Log Houses in Grainger County," 168.

Chapter Four

1. Burns, *Blount County*, 63.
2. Ibid., 15.
3. For a discussion of the characteristics of "I" houses and their locations in the United States, see Kniffen, "Folk Housing," 549–77.
4. Burns, *Blount County*, 58–67.
5. Killebrew, *Resources of Tennessee*, 557.
6. Saunders, "East Tennessee," 202.
7. Ibid.
8. J.E. Prater, Louisville, Tenn., interview, June 1984.

9. *The Watchman* (Maryville, Tenn.), 24 Apr. 1883; *East Tennessean* (Maryville, Tenn.), 17 Sept. 1883.
10. *Maryville Times*, 19 May 1886.
11. Ibid., 2 Jan. 1889.
12. Ibid., 7 Aug. 1889.
13. Ibid., 17 Feb. 1886.
14. Ibid., 28 Aug. 1889.
15. Ibid., 6 Nov. 1889.
16. Ibid., 23 Apr. 1890; 21 Jan., 2 Feb., 18 Feb. 1891.
17. Ibid., 18 May 1892; 3 Jan., 31 Jan., 21 Feb., 28 Feb., 4 Apr., 9 May, 31 Oct., 21 Nov., 28 Nov. 1894.
18. Prater, interview; James T. Gamble, Knoxville, Tenn., interview, July 1984. Although 96 years old in 1984, Gamble's memory for details of his youth was impressive. For example, he not only remembered that the extant four-crib log barn on the old Gamble farm near Wildwood was built in 1895, but he also vividly described Milford DeArmond, the elderly barn carpenter.

Chapter Five

1. Killebrew, *Resources of Tennessee*, 463.
2. A.W. Hawkins, *Hand-Book of Tennessee* (Knoxville: Whig and Chronicle Steam Book and Job Printing Office, 1882), 89.
3. *The Watchman*, Apr. 1882.
4. George E. Brewer, "History of Coosa County, Alabama" (manuscript in Alabama Department of Archives and History, Montgomery), quoted in Frank Lawrence Owsley, *Plain Folk of the Old South* (Baton Rouge: Louisiana State Univ. Press, 1949), 106–107. Cooperative work efforts among neighbors in Blount County are described in Shields, *Cades Coves Story*, 34–37.
5. Mary White, Walland, Tenn., interview, Nov. 1982.
6. For example, the Cal Lane house, in the Walland area, was built c. 1880 by a well-known Blount County house carpenter, "Snakey" John Martin.
7. Historical information on water-powered sawmills is included in Fred H. Gilman, "History of the Development of Sawmill and Woodworking Machinery," *Mississippi Valley Lumberman* 36 (1 Feb. 1895):59–61;

Henry C. Mercer, *Ancient Carpenter Tools* (Doylestown, Pa.: Bucks County Historical Society, 5th ed., 1975), 25–30; John W. Oliver, *History of American Technology* (New York: Ronald Press, 1956), 26–28; and Charles E. Peterson, "Sawdust Trail," *Bulletin of the Association for Preservation Technology* 5, no. 2 (1973):84–87. A good regional treatment of waterpowered sawmills in the United States is Donald A. Hutslar, "Ohio Waterpowered Sawmills," *Ohio History* 84 (1975):6–58.

8. Vic Weals, "Idle Mill Gone with the Wind," *Knoxville Journal*, 29 Dec. 1977, and "It's an Old, Old Road to Warner Martin's Mill," *Knoxville Journal*, 15 Dec. 1977; Inez E. Burns, *Blount County*, 217–18; Louise Lanstrath Messler, "Cloyd's Creek," *Maryville Times*, 8 June 1942.

9. Ibid.

10. U.S. Bureau of the Census, *Eighth Census of the United States: 1860* (Washington, D.C.: 1864).

11. Graeme Wynn, *Timber Colony* (Tornoto: Univ. of Toronto Press, 1981), 87.

12. Roy B. Clarkson, "Mountain Logging in the Appalachians at the Turn of the Century," *Southern Lumberman* 233 (15 Dec. 1976):118.

13. William B. Lenoir, *History of Sweetwater Valley, Tennessee* (Baltimore: Regional Publishing Co., 1976; reprint of 1916 ed.).

14. Ibid., 162.

15. Historical information on the pit or whip saw is provided in Gilman, "Sawmill and Woodworking Machinery," 59, and Mercer, *Ancient Carpenter Tools*, 21–25.

16. "Saws of several patterns were used; the most common had a blade six or seven feet in length": Nollie Hickman, *Mississippi Harvest* (University: Univ. of Mississippi Press, 1962), 16.

17. Clarkson, "Mountain Logging," 118.

18. Inez Burns, "Settlement and Early History of the Coves of Blount County, Tennessee," *East Tennessee Historical Society's Publications* 24 (1952):55.

19. Vic Weals, "Each Member Had a Hand in Building the Stratton Home," *Knoxville Journal*, 29 Dec. 1983.

20. Vic Weals, "Strattons Left Name on Mountain," *Knoxville Journal*, 22 Dec. 1983.

21. Timber frame construction descended from European half-timber construction, in which the wall spaces between the posts and braces

were filled with a nogging, usually brick. Half-timber construction was transferred to the Eastern Seaboard areas of colonial America, but eventually weatherboarding was added and the nogging generally omitted from American houses.

Timber frame construction in 19th-century Tennessee is described by Patrick, *Architecture in Tennessee*, 16–30, although Patrick prefers the term "braced frame construction" rather than "timber frame construction." Other discussions and illustrations of timber frame are found in Carl W. Condit, *American Building* (Chicago: Univ. of Chicago Press, 2d ed., 1982), 2–25; Paul E. Buchanan, "The Eighteenth-Century Frame Houses of Tidewater, Virginia," in *Building Early America*, ed. Charles E. Peterson (Radnor, Pa.: Chilton, 1976), 54–73; Dell Upton, "Traditional Timber Framing," in *Material Culture of the Wooden Age*, ed. Brooke Hindle (Tarrytown, N.Y.: Sleepy Hollow Press, 1981), 35–93.

22. Gerald W. Kline, Robert A. Pace, and Linda Carnes, *An Archeological Reconnaissance Survey of the Proposed Piegon Forge Park, Sevier County, Tennessee* (Knoxville: Dept. of Anthropology, Univ. of Tennessee, 1983); Weals, "It's an Old, Old Road," and "Idle Mill Gone with the Wind."

23. Patrick, *Architecture in Tennessee*, 19, 21.

24. Ibid., 18.

25. U.S. Bureau of the Census, *Ninth Census of the United States, 1870*, Manuscript Schedules of Population for Blount County.

26. Ibid.

27. Lee H. Nelson, "Nail Chronology as an Aid to Dating Old Buildings," American Assoc. for State and Local History Technical Leaflet 48, *History News* 24 (Nov. 1968). Although much remains to be learned about the history of nail production in the U.S., the best sources on the subject are Lee H. Nelson and Henry C. Mercer, *The Dating of Old Houses* (Doylestown, Pa.: Bucks County Historical Society, 1976), 2–10, and Mercer, *Ancient Carpenter Tools*, 235–60.

28. Patrick, *Architecture in Tennessee*, 26.

29. Morris, *Tennessee Gazeteer*, 129.

30. *Knoxville Register*, 30 Apr. 1834.

31. *Knoxville Register*, 13 Jan. 1841.

32. *Knoxville Register*, 29 June 1850.

33. *East Tennessean* (Maryville, Tenn.), 26 Oct. 1855.

34. *Brownlow's* (Knoxville), 21 Mar. 1857.
35. *Knoxville Register*, 13 Jan. 1841.
36. *Knoxville Register*, 30 May 1849.
37. Frontier life and economy in East Tennessee are described in William Flinn Rogers, "Life in East Tennessee Near the End of Eighteenth Century," *East Tennessee Historical Society's Pulications* 1 (1929): 27–42; and Thomas Perkins Abernethy, *From Frontier to Plantation in Tennessee* (Chapel Hill: Univ. of North Carolina Press, 1932), 144–163. The character and development of agriculture in Tennessee in the late antebellum period are discussed in Blanche Henry Clark, *The Tennessee Yeomen* (Nashville: Vanderbilt Univ. Press, 1942); Frank L. Owsley and Harriet C. Owsley, "The Economic Structure of Rural Tennessee, 1850–1860," *Journal of Southern History* 8 (1942):161–82; Frank Owsley, *Plain Folk of the Old South*.
38. Clark, *Tennessee Yeomen*, 1–7.
39. Ibid., 8.
40. Donald W. Buckwalter, "Effects of Early Nineteenth Century Transportation Disadvantage on the Agriculture of Eastern Tennessee," *Southeastern Geographer* 27, no. 1 (1987):18–37.
41. Clark, *Tennessee Yeomen*, 9, 27.
42. Frank Owsley and Harriet Owsley, "Rural Tennessee," 176.
43. Killebrew, *Resources of Tennessee*, 351, 353.
44. Ibid., 353.
45. Ibid., 354.
46. *The Republican* (Maryville, Tenn.), 26 Feb. 1870. Advertisements included the following statements:

(1) "I have a large lot of Leather, such as Sole, Upper, Kip, Calf, Goat Skins ... which I will exchange for Bark, Hides, Corn, Bacon, &c."

(2) "Wanted! Wanted! Old Iron, dry bones, and rags, for which the market price will be paid in merchandise and all kinds of tin ware."

(3) "Sash, Blinds, Doors, Mouldings, Tables ... Window and Door Frames ... Job Turning and Sawing ... Good Lumber, such as Pine, Poplar, Walnut, Gum, and Cherry, taken in exchange."

(4) "New Fall and Winter Goods ... For Cash or Produce."

47. Edmund Cody Burnett, "Shingle Making on the Lesser Waters of the Big Creek of the French Broad River," *Agricultural History* 20 (1946): 232–33.

48. Saunders, "East Tennessee," 202.

49. Shields, *Cades Cove Story*, 18–37.

50. Ibid., 18.

51. Dunn, *Cades Cove*, 73–74; Killebrew, *Resources of Tennessee*, 355.

52. The Tennessee River begins at Knoxville, at the confluence of the Holston and French Broad rivers, and flows southward through East Tennessee. In the 19th century, however, the name Tennessee River was used only south of where the Little Tennessee River empties into the stream. Between Knoxville and the Little Tennessee River, the stream was called the Holston River. Thus Louisville was a port on the Holston River during the 19th century.

53. A.H. Love, "The History of Louisville, Blount County, Tennessee" (manuscript in Special Collections, Univ. of Tennessee Library, written 1922).

54. Lewis Cecil Gray, *History of Agriculture in the Southern United States to 1860*, v. 2 (Gloucester, Mass.: Peter Smith, 1958), 816.

55. Buckwalter, "Transportation Disadvantage," 35; Eller, *Miners, Millhands, and Mountaineers*, 21; Edmund Cody Burnett, "Hog Raising and Hog Driving in the Region of the French Broad River," *Agricultural History* 20 (1946):86–103; Wilma Dykeman, *The French Broad* (Knoxville: Univ. of Tennessee Press, 1955), 140–42.

Chapter Six

1. *U.S. Census of Agriculture*, 1850, 1860, 1870, 1880, 1890, and 1900.

2. Thomas H. Freeman, *An Economic History of Tennessee* (Nashville: Tennessee State Planning Commission, 1965), 25.

3. Saunders, "East Tennessee," 202; Durwood Clay Dunn, "Cades Cove During the Nineteenth Century" (Ph.D. diss., Univ. of Tennessee, Knoxville, 1976), 60, 64.

4. Burns, *Blount County*, 235–37.

5. Love, "History of Louisville," 12.

6. U.S. Bureau of the Census, *Ninth Census of the United States, 1870*, Manuscript Schedules of Population for Blount County.

7. Ibid.

8. Jordan, *Texas Log Buildings*, 5.

9. Pauline Massengill DeFriece and Frank B. Williams, Jr., "Rocky

Mount: The Cobb-Massengill Home, First Capitol of the Territory of the United States South of the River Ohio," *Tennessee Historical Quarterly* 25, no. 2 (1966):119–34; quote, 131.

10. Messler, "Cloyd's Creek."

11. Adele McKenzie, "At Brick Mill—Six Generations of Henrys," *Maryville-Alcoa Daily Times*, 25 Feb. 1972.

12. Killebrew, *Resources of Tennessee*, 608.

13. *Maryville Times*, 9 Nov. 1887. The newspaper editor appears to have been promoting the "New South" industrial development philosophy, which advocated industrialization based on local resources and labor, plus outside capital. For a discussion of the New South philosophy and its impact on Appalachia, see Eller, *Miners, Millhands, and Mountaineers*, 39–85.

14. Burns, *Blount County*, 323–24.

Chapter Seven

1. Eller, *Miners, Millhands, and Mountaineers*, 26; Zelinsky, "Log House in Georgia," 181.

2. U.S. Bureau of the Census, *Ninth Census of the United States: 1870* (Washington, D.C.: 1872), and *Tenth Census of the United States: 1880* (Washington, D.C.: 1883).

3. Killebrew, *Resources of Tennessee*, 463.

4. Compiled from *10th U.S. Census: 1880*; Burns, *Blount County*, 221–22, 229–31; Robert S. Lambert, "Logging on the Little River, 1890–1940," *East Tennessee Historical Society's Publications* 33 (1961):32–42; various issues of *Northwestern Lumberman* (Chicago); *Blount County Democrat* (Maryville); *The Watchman* (Maryville); *East Tennessee News* (Maryville); *Maryville Times*; *Maryville Index*.

5. J. Richards, *A Treatsie on the Construction and Operation of Woodworking Machines* (London: E. & F.N. Spon, 1872), edited selections in *Forest History* 9, no. 4 (Jan. 1966):16–23; quote, 22.

6. Nathan Rosenberg, "America's Rise to Woodworking Leadership," in *America's Wooden Age: Aspects of Its Early Technology*, ed. Brooke Hindle (Tarrytown, N.Y.: Sleepy Hollow Restorations, 1975), 46; Norman Ball, "Circular Saws and the History of Technology," *Bulletin of the Association for Preservation Technology*, 7 (1975):80, 84.

7. Richards, "Woodworking Machines," 22.
8. *The Republican*, 30 May 1874.
9. *East Tennessean*, 19 Feb. 1858.
10. A steam sawmill was in existence in Nashville some years before 1831; Patrick, *Architecture in Tennessee*, 23.
11. *Brownlow's*, 16 Dec. 1854.
12. Killebrew, *Resources of Tennessee*, 463.
13. *10th U.S. Census: 1880*.
14. Meade Milton Johnson, *Southern Families: The Descendants of Elkanah and Catherine Johnson* (New Canaan, Conn.: privately published, 1977), 7–8; *Maryville Index*, 4 June 1879; *The Watchman*, 19 Apr. 1882.
15. *Maryville Times*, 24 Mar. 1886; *Maryville Record*, 22 July 1904.
16. Ethel Cox Smith, Louisville, Tenn., interview, June 1984.
17. Prater, interview.
18. Mrs. W.O. Laffell, Louisville, Tenn., interview, June 1984.
19. *Maryville Index*, 20 Nov. 1878.
20. Ibid., 17 July 1878.
21. Ibid., 23 Oct. 1889.
22. Compiled from *Maryville Times*, 1890–97.
23. Ibid., 17 Mar. 1886.
24. Ibid., 24 Mar., 21 Apr. 1886.
25. Ibid., 17 Jan. 1894; 27 Feb. 1896.
26. Nellie Smith, Maryville, Tenn., interview, June 1985.
27. Bessie Gamble, Ellejoy, Tenn., interview, Apr. 1984.
28. Bessie Pickens Garrison, Seymour, Tenn., interview, May 1984.
29. Shields, *Cades Cove Story*, 58.
30. *Maryville Record*, 20 May, 3 June, 10 June, 24 June 1904.
31. Ibid., 3 June 1904.
32. Ibid., 10 June 1904.
33. Burns, *Blount County*, 230; Lambert, "Logging on Little River," 33.
34. The history of railroad construction in Blount County is described in Burns, *Blount County*, 235–37.
35. The name of the Knoxville and Charleston Railroad was changed to the Knoxville and Augusta in 1879; see ibid., 236.
36. Lambert, "Logging on Little River," 33.
37. Ibid.; Burns, *Blount County*, 230.

38. *The Democrat*, 15 Apr. 1882.
39. *The Watchman*, 21 June, 28 June 1882.
40. *Blount County Democrat*, 20 Jan. 1883; *East Tennessee News*, 17 Sept. 1883; *The Watchman*, 24 Apr. 1883.
41. *Maryville Times*, 17 Feb. 1886.
42. Ibid., 6 Jan. 1886, reported that T.R. Vineyard, "the enterprising saw mill man," was doing custom work in the Ellejoy area.
43. *Maryville Times*, 21 Apr. 1886.
44. Prater, interview.
45. *Maryville Times*, 26 Mar. 1896.
46. Ibid., 9 May 1896.
47. Ibid., 11 Feb. 1891.
48. Ibid., 16 Apr. 1890; Feb. 25, April 1, 1891.
49. Ibid., 14 Jan. 1891.
50. Ibid., 29 Apr. 1891.
51. Ibid., 25 May, 19 Oct. 1892.
52. Burns, *Blount County*, 230.
53. Ibid.; Lambert, "Logging on Little River," 36.
54. Burns, *Blount County*, 230.
55. Howard Sparks, quoted in Vic Weals, "Cove Lumber Plentiful—Road to Market Steep," *Knoxville Journal*, 7 Jan. 1982. According to Sparks, prior to the construction of the Little River Railroad, some valuable lumber, particularly cherry, was sawed at the Cable waterpowered sash sawmill and hauled to a coffin factory at Maryville. After construction of the railroad to Townsend, the haul was shortened but was still long enough that cheaper lumber, such as yellow pine, would not pay the cost of transporting it. Much of the commerical lumbering in Cades Cove was devoted to the sawing of white pine, which grew in abundance and sold for a relatively high price.
56. Dunn, *Cades Cove*, 226–27, 233; quote, 233.
57. Nellie Smith, interview.
58. M.B. McMahan II, *James McMahan, First from Dublin, Ireland, Patriot of the Revolutionary War* (Sevierville, Tenn.: M.B. McMahan, 1980), 10.

Chapter Eight

1. Solon Robinson, "How to Build Balloon Frames," *New York Tribune*, 18 Jan. 1855.

2. The origin of the balloon frame is discussed in Sigfried Giedion, *Space, Time, and Architecture* (Cambridge, Mass.: MIT Press, 1967, 5th ed.), 352–53; Walker Field, Jr., "A Reexamination into the Invention of the Balloon Frame," *Journal of the Society of Architectural Historians* 2 (Oct. 1942):3–29; Daniel J. Boorstin, *The Americans: The National Experience* (New York: Random House, 1965), 149, 460; Paul E. Sprague, "The Origin of Balloon Framing," *Journal of the Society of Architectural Historians* 40 (Dec. 1981):311–19; Condit, *American Building*, 43; Leland M. Roth, ed., *America Builds: Source Documents in American Architecture and Planning* (New York: Harper and Row, 1983), 53.

3. Boorstin, *The Americans*, 149–52; Condit, *American Building*, 43–45; Roth, *America Builds*, 53.

4. Patrick, *Architecture in Tennessee*, 29.

5. Solon Robinson, "Balloon Frames," 6.

6. Dianne Tebbetts, "Traditional Houses of Independence County, Arkansas," *Pioneer America* 10, no. 1 (1978):43.

7. Walter R. Nelson, "Some Examples of Plank House Construction and Their Origin," *Pioneer America* no. 1 (July 1969):18–29.

8. T. Ritchie, "Plankwall Framing, a Modern Wall Construction with an Ancient History," *Journal of the Society of Architectural Historians* 30 (1971):66–70; Robert Jensen, "Board and Batten Siding and the Balloon Frame: Their Incompatibility in the Nineteenth Century," *Journal of the Society of Architectural Historians* 30 (1971):41.

9. Jensen, "Board and Batten Siding and Balloon Frame," 41–42.

10. Ella Enslow, *Schoolhouse in the Foothills* (New York: Simon and Schuster, 1935), 35–36; A.E. Scott, "A Visit to Mitchell and Roan Mountains," *Appalachia* 4 (Dec. 1884):15; M.B. McMahan, *James McMahan First*, 12; Tebbetts, "Traditional Houses," 43; E. Raymond Evans, "The Strip House in Tennessee Folk-Architecture," *Tennessee Folklore Society Bulletin* 42 (Dec. 1976):163–66; Eller, *Miners, Millhands, and Mountaineers*, 27.

11. Eller, *Miners, Millhands, and Mountaineers*, 27.

12. Steve Mitchell, Donald R. Brown, and Michael L. Swanda, in "Board Shanty: Box Construction in White County, Arkansas," *Pioneer*

America Society Transactions 10 (1987):9–16, found (p. 11) that most box houses in White County, Arkansas, were associated with the rural poor, especially tenants, but that several such houses were built by persons "of prosperity and relative affluence."

13. Prater, interview.
14. Shirley Hall, Greenback, Tenn., interview, Apr. 1984.
15. McMahan, 12.
16. Charles E. Martin, *Hollybush* (Knoxville: Univ. of Tennessee Press, 1984), 92.
17. Scott, "Mitchell and Roan Mountains," 15.
18. Enslow, *Schoolhouse in the Foothills*, 35–36.
19. Martin, *Hollybush*, 93.
20. Mitchell, Brown, and Swanda, "Board Shanty," 11.

Chapter Nine

1. Boorstin, *The Americans*, 148.
2. Robert N. Van Benthuysen, Jr., "The Sequent Occupance of Tellico Plains, Tennessee" (M.S. thesis, Univ. of Tennessee, 1951), 31–42.
3. Ibid., 39.
4. Peirce F. Lewis, "Reading the Landscape," 23.
5. Ibid.
6. Jordan, *Texas Log Buildings*, 5, 27, 29.
7. Zelinsky, "Log House in Georgia," 181.
8. Pillsbury, "Pennsylvania Culture Region," 29.

Bibliography

Books, Pamphlets, and Printed Government Documents

Abernethy, Thomas Perkins. *From Frontier to Plantation in Tennessee.* Chapel Hill: University of North Carolina Press, 1932.

Adkins, Howard G., Steve Ewing, and Chester E. Zimolzak, eds. *West Virginia and Appalachia: Selected Readings.* Dubuque, Iowa: Kendall-Hunt, 1977.

Allison, John. *Dropped Stitches in Tennessee History.* Nashville: Marshall and Bruce, 1897.

Andrews, Ralph W. *This Was Sawmilling.* Seattle, Wash.: Superior Publishing, 1957.

Arnow, Harriette Simpson. *Seedtime on the Cumberland.* New York: Macmillan, 1960.

Ayres, H.B. and W.W. Ashe. *The Southern Appalachian Forests.* Washington, D.C.: U.S. Government Printing Office, 1905.

Blount County Historic Trust. *Back Home in Blount County.* Maryville, Tenn.: Blount County Historic Trust, 1986.

Boorstin, Daniel J. *The Americans: The National Experience.* New York: Random House, 1965.

Bowman, Elizabeth Skaggs. *Land of High Horizons.* Kingsport, Tenn.: Southern Publishers, 1938.

Brunskill, R.W. *Illustrated Handbook of Vernacular Architecture.* London: Faber and Faber, 1971.

Brunvand, Jan H., ed. *The Study of American Folklore.* New York: Norton, 1965.

Bryant, Ralph Clement. *Lumber: Its Manufacture and Distribution.* New York: Wiley, 1922.

Buckingham, J.S. *The Slave States of America.* New York: Negro Universities Press, 1968. Reprint of original 1842 edition.

Burns, Inez E. *History of Blount County, Tennessee, From War Trail to Landing Strip, 1795–1955.* Nashville: Benson Printing Co., 1957.

Callahan, North. *Smoky Mountain Country.* New York: Duell, Sloan and Pearce, 1952.

Campbell, John C. *The Southern Highlander and His Homeland.* Lexington: University Press of Kentucky, 1969. Reprint of 1921 edition.

Carter, Thomas, and Bernard L. Herman. *Perspectives in Vernacular Architecture, III.* Columbia: University of Missouri Press, 1989.

Case, Earl C. *The Valley of East Tennessee.* Nashville: Tennessee Division of Geology, 1925.

Clark, Blanche Henry. *The Tennessee Yeomen, 1840–1860.* Nashville: Vanderbilt University Press, 1942.

Condit, Carl W. *American Building.* Chicago: University of Chicago Press, 2d ed., 1982.

Corlew, Robert E., Stanley J. Folmsbee, and Enoch L. Mitchell. *Tennessee—A Short History.* Knoxville: University of Tennessee Press, 1969.

Couch, W.T., ed. *Culture in the South.* Chapel Hill: University of North Carolina Press, 1934.

Crane, Sophie, and Paul Crane. *Tennessee Taproots.* Old Hickory, Tenn.: Earle-Shields Publishers, 1976.

Deardorff, Jeffry L. *Blount County: 1990.* Maryville, Tenn.: Blount County Regional Planning Commission, 1976.

Dennett, John Richard. *The South As It Is: 1865–66.* New York: Viking, 1965.

Dornbush, Charles E. *Pennsylvania German Barns: Twenty-First Yearbook of the Pennsylvania German Folklore Society.* Allentown, Pa.: Pennsylvania German Folklore Society, 1955.

Dorson, Richard M., ed. *Folklore and Folklife.* Chicago: University of Chicago Press, 1972.

Dunn, Durwood. *Cades Cove: The Life and Death of a Southern Appalachian Community, 1818–1937.* Knoxville: University of Tennessee Press, 1988.

Dykeman, Wilma. *The French Broad.* New York: Rinehart, 1955.

Eaton, Allen H. *Handicrafts of the Southern Highlands.* New York: Russell Sage Foundation, 1937.

Eaton, Clement. *The Growth of Southern Civilization, 1790–1860.* New York: Harper and Brothers, 1961.

———. *A History of the Old South*. New York: Macmillan, 2d ed., 1966.

Elder, Joe A., et al. *Soil Survey of Blount County, Tennessee*. Washington, D.C.: U.S. Government Printing Office, 1959.

Eller, Ronald D. *Miners, Millhands, and Mountaineers: Industrialization of the Appalachian South, 1880–1930*. Knoxville: University of Tennessee Press, 1982.

Enslow, Ella. *Schoolhouse in the Foothills*. New York: Simon and Schuster, 1935.

Featherstonhaugh, G.W. *Excursion through the Slave States*. London: John Murray, 1844.

Fitch, James Marston. *American Building: The Historical Forces that Shaped It*. Boston: Houghton Mifflin, 2d ed., 1966.

Ford, Thomas R., ed. *The Southern Appalachian Region: A Survey*. Lexington: University Press of Kentucky, 1962.

Fox, John Ballenger. *The People of Tennessee*. Knoxville: University of Tennessee Press, 1949.

Freeman, Thomas H., IV. *An Economic History of Tennessee*. Nashville: Tennessee State Planning Commission, 1965.

Frome, Michael. *Strangers in High Places*. Garden City, N.Y.: Doubleday, 1966. Reprint ed. Knoxville: University of Tennessee Press, 1980.

Gibson, James R., ed. *European Settlement and Development in North America*. Toronto: University of Toronto Press, 1978.

Glass, Joseph W. *The Pennsylvania Culture Region: A View from the Barn*. Ann Arbor, Mich.: UMI Research Press, 1986.

Glassie, Henry. *Pattern in the Material Folk Culture of the Eastern United States*. Philadelphia: University of Pennsylvania Press, 1968.

———. *Folk Housing in Middle Virginia*. Knoxville: University of Tennessee Press, 1975.

Goodspeed, Weston A. *History of Tennessee*. Nashville: Goodspeed Publishing, 1887.

Gray, Lewis Cecil. *History of Agriculture in the Southern United States to 1860*. 2 vols. Gloucester, Mass.: Peter Smith, 1958.

Greve, Jeanette S. *The Story of Gatlinburg*. Strasburg, Va.: Shenandoah Publishing, 1931.

Hall, C.W. *Threescore Years and Ten*. Cincinnati, Ohio: Elm Street Printing, 1884.

Hart, John Fraser. *The Look of the Land*. Englewood Cliffs, N.J.: Prentice-Hall, 1975.

Hawk, Emory Q. *Economic History of the South*. New York: Prentice-Hall, 1934.

Hawkins, A.W. *Hand-Book of Tennessee*. Knoxville: Whig and Chronicle Steam Book and Job Printing Office, 1882.

Herman, Bernard L. *Architecture and Rural Life in Central Delaware, 1700–1900*. Knoxville: University of Tennessee Press, 1987.

Hickman, Nollie. *Mississippi Harvest: Lumbering in the Long-Leaf Pine Belt, 1840–1915*. University, Miss.: University of Mississippi Press, 1962.

Hicks, Nannie Lee. *Historic Treasure Spots of Knox County, Tennessee*. Knoxville: Simon Harris Chapter, Daughters of the American Revolution, 1964.

———. *The John Adair Section of Knox County, Tennessee*. Knoxville: Nannie Lee Hicks and the Nocturne Garden Club, 1968.

Hilliard, Sam B. *Hog Meat and Hoe Cake: Food Supply in the Old South*. Carbondale: Southern Illinois University Press, 1972.

Hindle, Brooke, ed. *America's Wooden Age: Aspects of its Early Technology*. Tarrytown, N.Y.: Sleepy Hollow Restoration, 1975.

———, ed. *Material Culture of the Wooden Age*. Tarrytown, N.Y.: Sleepy Hollow Press, 1981.

Holt, Edgar A. *Claiborne County*. Memphis, Tenn.: Memphis State University Press, 1981.

Hoskins, Katherine B. *Anderson County*. Memphis, Tenn.: Memphis State University Press, 1979.

Hughes, Thomas. *Rugby, Tennessee*. London: Macmillan, 1881.

Imlay, Gilbert. *A Topographical Description of the Western Territory of North America*. London: F. DeBrett, 3d ed., 1797.

Jackson, John Brinckerhoff. *Discovering the Vernacular Landscape*. New Haven, Conn.: Yale University Press, 1984.

Johnson, Amandus. *Swedish Settlement on the Delaware*. Appleton, N.Y.: University of Pennsylvania Publications, 1911.

Johnson, Meade Milton. *Southern Families: The Descendents of Elkanah and Mary Catherine Johnson*. New Canaan, Conn.: Privately Published, 1977.

Jordan, Terry G. *Texas Log Buildings: A Folk Architecture.* Austin: University of Texas Press, 1978.

———. *American Log Buildings.* Chapel Hill: University of North Carolina Press, 1985.

Jordan, Terry G., and Matti Kaups. *The American Backwoods Frontier: An Ethnic and Ecological Interpretation.* Baltimore: Johns Hopkins University Press, 1989.

Jordan, Terry G., and Lester Rowntree. *The Human Mosaic: A Thematic Introduction to Cultural Geography.* San Francisco: Canfield Press, 1976.

Kephart, Horace. *Our Southern Highlanders.* Knoxville: University of Tennessee Press, 1976. Reprint of original 1913 edition.

Kercheval, Samuel. *A History of the Valley of Virginia.* Strasburg, Va.: Shenandoah Publishing House, 4th ed., 1925.

Killebrew, J.B. *Introduction to the Resources of Tennessee.* Nashville: Tavel, Eastman and Howell, 1874.

Kline, Gerald W., Robert Al Pace, and Linda Carnes. *An Archaeological Reconnaisance Survey of the Proposed Pigeon Forge Park, Sevier County, Tennessee.* Knoxville: Midsouth Anthropological Research Center, Department of Anthropology, University of Tennessee, 1983.

Lair, E.A. *Carpentry.* New York: McGraw-Hill, 2d ed., 1953.

Lenoir, William B. *History of Sweetwater Valley, Tennessee.* Baltimore, Md.: Regional Publishing Co., 1976. Reprint of original 1916 edition.

Leuthold, Frank O. *Population, Migration, and Natural Increase Trends in Tennessee from 1930 to 1980.* Bulletin 608, Agricultural Experiment Station. Knoxville: University of Tennessee, 1982.

Lillard, Richard G. *The Great Forest.* New York: DeCapo Press, 1973.

Livingood, James W. *Hamilton County.* Memphis, Tenn.: Memphis State University Press, 1981.

Long, Amos, Jr. *The Pennsylvania German Family Farm.* Breinigsville, Pa.: Pennsylvania German Society, 1972.

McAlester, Virginia, and Lee McAlester. *A Field Guide to American Houses.* New York: Knopf, 1984.

McDonald, James J. *Life in Old Virginia,* Norfolk: Old Virginia Publishing Company, 1907.

McDonald, Michael J., and William Bruce Wheeler. *Knoxville, Tennes-*

see: *Continuity and Change in an Appalachian City.* Knoxville: University of Tennessee Press, 1983.

McMahan, M.B., II. *James McMahan First, From Dublin, Ireland, Patriot of the Revolutionary War.* Sevierville, Tenn.: M.B. McMahan, 1980.

McMurray, J.H., ed. *Social Survey of Blount County, 1930.* Maryville, Tenn.: Maryville College, 1930.

Madden, Robert R., and T. Russell Jones. *Walker Sisters Home, Historic Structures Report, Part II, and Furnishing Study.* Washington: U.S. Department of Interior, National Park Service, 1969.

―――. *Mountain Home: The Walker Family Farmstead, Great Smoky Mountains National Park.* Washington, D.C.: U.S. Department of Interior, National Park Service, 1977.

Marshall, Howard Wight. *Folk Architecture in Little Dixie: A Regional Culture in Missouri.* Columbia: University of Missouri Press, 1981.

Martin, Charles E. *Hollybush: Folk Building and Social Change in an Appalachian Community.* Knoxville: University of Tennessee Press, 1984.

Mason, Robert Lindsay. *The Lure of the Great Smokies.* Boston: Houghton Mifflin, 1927.

Maxwell, Robert S., and Robert D. Baker. *Sawdust Empire.* College Station: Texas A & M University Press, 1983.

Meinig, D.W. *The Shaping of America: A Geographical Perspective on Five Hundred Years of History.* New Haven, Conn.: Yale University Press, 1986.

―――, ed. *The Interpretation of Ordinary Landscapes.* New York: Oxford University Press, 1979.

Mercer, Henry C. *The Dating of Old Houses.* Doylestown, Pa.: Bucks County Historical Society, 1976. Reprinted from *Bucks County Historical Society Papers* 5 (1926): 536-49.

―――. *The Origin of Log Houses in the United States.* Doylestown, Pa.: Bucks County Historical Society, 1976. Originally published in *Bucks County Historical Society Papers* 5 (1926): 568-83.

―――. *Ancient Carpenter Tools.* Doylestown, Pa.: Bucks County Historical Society, 5th ed., 1975.

Michaux, F.A. *Travels to the West of the Allegheny Mountains.* London: B. Crosby and J.P. Hughes, 1805. Reprinted in *Early Western Travels,*

1748–1846, edited by Reuben Gold Thwaites, vol. 3, 105.306. Cleveland, Ohio: Arthur Clark Company, 1904.

Miles, Emma Bell. *The Spirit of the Mountains.* New York: J. Pott, 1905. Reprint ed. Knoxville: University of Tennessee Press, 1975.

Mitchell, Robert D. *Commercialism and Frontier: Perspectives on the Early Shenandoah Valley.* Charlottesville: University Press of Virginia, 1977.

Mitchell, Robert D., and Paul A. Groves, eds. *North America: The Historical Geography of a Changing Continent.* Totowa, N.J.: Rowman and Littlefield, 1987.

Mitchell, Robert D., and Milton B. Newton. *The Appalachian Frontier: Views from the East and the Southwest.* London: Institute of British Geographers, Historical Geography Research Series, no. 21, 1988.

Moffett, Marian, and Lawrence Wodehouse. *The Cantilever Barn in East Tennessee.* Knoxville: School of Architecture, University of Tennessee, 1984.

Montell, William Lynwood. *Don't Go Up Kettle Creek: Verbal Legacy of the Upper Cumberland.* Knoxville: University of Tennessee Press, 1983.

Morris, Eastin. *The Tennessee Gazetteer.* Nashville: W. Hasell Hunt and Company, 1834.

Muir, John. *A Thousand-Mile Walk to the Gulf.* Boston: Houghton Mifflin, 1916.

Noble, Allen G. *Wood, Brick, and Stone: The North American Settlement Landscape*, 2 vols. Amherst: University of Massachusetts Press, 1984.

Oliver, John W. *History of American Technology.* New York: Ronald Press, 1956.

Olmsted, Frederick Law. *A Journey in the Back Country.* New York: Burt Franklin, 1970. Reprint of 1860 edition.

Owsley, Frank Lawrence. *Plain Folk of the Old South.* Baton Rouge: Louisiana State University Press, 1949.

Paine, Thomas H. *Handbook of Tennessee.* Nashville: McQuiddy Printing Co., 1903.

Parkins, A.E. *The South: Its Economic-Geographic Development.* New York: John Wiley, 1938.

Patrick, James. *Architecture in Tennessee, 1768–1897.* Knoxville: University of Tennessee Press, 1981.

Peattle, Roderick, ed. *The Great Smokies and the Blue Ridge.* New York: Vanguard, 1943.

Peterson, Charles E., ed. *Building Early America: Contributions toward the History of a Great Industry.* Radnor, Pa.: Chilton, 1976.

Powell, Levi W. *Who Are These Mountain People? An Intimate Historical Account of Southern Appalachia.* New York: Exposition Press, 1966.

Pursell, Carroll W., Jr., ed. *Technology in America.* Cambridge, Mass.: MIT Press, 1981.

Raine, James Watt. *The Land of Saddlebags: A Study of the Mountain People of Appalachia.* Richmond, Va.: Presbyterian Committee of Publication, 1924.

Raitz, Karl B., and Richard Ulack. *Appalachia: A Regional Geography.* Boulder, Colo.: Westview, 1984.

Ralph, Julian. *Dixie.* New York: Harper and Brothers, 1896.

Raulston, J. Leonard, and James W. Livingood. *Sequatchie, A Story of the Southern Cumberlands.* Knoxville: University of Tennessee Press, 1974.

Reynolds, R.V. and Albert H. Pierson. *Lumber Cut of the United States, 1870–1920.* U.S. Department of Agriculture Bulletin 1119. Washington, D.C.: U.S. Government Printing Office, 1923.

Richardson, Miles, ed. *The Human Mirror.* Baton Rouge: Louisiana State University Press, 1974.

Riedl, Norbert F.; Donald B. Ball; and Anthony P. Cavender. *A Survey of Traditional Architecture and Related Material Folk Culture Patterns in the Normandy Reservoir, Coffee County, Tennessee.* Knoxville: Tennessee Valley Authority, 1976.

Roberts, Warren E. *Log Buildings of Southern Indiana.* Bloomington, Ind.: Trickster Press, 1985.

Roth, Leland M., ed. *America Builds: Source Documents in American Architecture and Planning.* New York: Harper and Row, 1983.

Rouse, Parke, Jr. *Planters and Pioneers: Life in Colonial Virginia.* New York: Hastings House, 1968.

Sauer, Carl Ortwin. *Land and Life: A Selection from the Writings of Carl Ortwin Sauer.* Berkeley: University of California Press, 1963.

Schwab, Eugene L., ed. *Travels in the Old South.* Vols. 1 and 2. Lexington: University Press of Kentucky, 1973.

Shackelford, Laurel, and Bill Weinberg. *Our Appalachia.* New York: Hill and Wang, 1977.

Sheppard, Muriel Early. *Cabins in the Laurel*. Chapel Hill: University of North Carolina Press, 1935.
Sherman, Mandel, and Thomas R. Henry. *Hollow Folk*. New York: Thomas Y. Crowell, 1933.
Shields, A. Randolph. *The Cades Cove Story*. Gatlinburg, Tenn.: Great Smoky Mountains Natural History Association, 1977.
Shoemaker, Alfred I., ed. *The Pennsylvania Barn*. Lancaster, Pa.: Pennsylvania Dutch Folklore Center, 1955.
Shurtleff, Harold R. *The Log Cabin Myth*. Gloucester, Mass.: Peter Smith, 1967.
Somers, Robert. *The Southern States Since the War, 1870–71*. University, Ala.: University of Alabama Press, 1965. Reprint of 1871 edition.
Spaulding, Arthur W. *The Men of the Mountains*. Nashville, Tenn.: Southern Publishing Association, 1915.
Stilgoe, John R. *Common Landscape of America, 1580 to 1845*. New Haven, Conn.: Yale University Press, 1982.
Stoner, Robert Douthat. *A Seed-Bed of the Republic*. Kingsport, Tenn.: Kingsport Press, 1962.
Swaim, Doug, ed. *Carolina Dwelling: Towards Preservation of Place, in Celebration of the North Carolina Vernacular Landscape*. Raleigh: School of Design, North Carolina State University, 1978.
Thompson, Samuel H. *The Highlanders of the South*. New York: Eaton and Mains, 1910.
Thornborough, Laura. *The Great Smoky Mountains*. New York: Thomas Y. Crowell, 1937.
Tindell, Ted. *Blount County: Communities We Live In*. Maryville, Tenn.: Marion R. Mangrum, 1973.
Turner, Frederick Jackson. *The Frontier in American History*. New York: Henry Holt, 1920.
Upton, Dell, ed. *America's Architectural Roots: Ethnic Groups that Built America*. Washington, D.C.: Preservation Press, 1986.
U.S. Bureau of the Census. *Seventh Census of the United States: 1850*. Washington, D.C., 1853.
———. *Eighth Census of the United States: 1860*. Washington, D.C., 1864.
———. *Ninth Census of the United States: 1870*. Washington, D.C., 1872.
———. *Tenth Census of the United States: 1880*. Washington, D.C. 1883.
———. *Eleventh Census of the United States: 1890*. Washington, D.C., 1895.

———. *Twelfth Census of the United States: 1900.* Washington, D.C. 1902.

U.S. Department of Agriculture. *The Farm-Housing Survey.* Miscellaneous publication no. 323. Washington, D.C., 1939.

Van Noppen, Ina W., and John J. Van Noppen. *Western North Carolina Since the Civil War.* Boone, N.C.: Appalachian Consortium Press, 1973.

Vance, Rupert B. *Human Geography of the South: A Study in Regional Resources and Human Adequacy.* Chapel Hill: University of North Carolina Press, 1935.

Wade, Richard C. *The Urban Frontier.* Chicago: University of Chicago Press, 1959.

Warner, Charles Dudley. *On Horseback: A Tour in Virginia, North Carolina and Tennessee.* Boston: Houghton Mifflin, 1888.

Weller, Jack E. *Yesterday's People.* Lexington: University Press of Kentucky, 1965.

Wells, Camille, ed. *Perspectives in Vernacular Architecture.* Columbia: University of Missouri Press, 1982.

———, ed. *Perspectives in Vernacular Architecture, II.* Columbia: University of Missouri Press, 1986.

Wertenbaker, Thomas Jefferson. *The Founding of American Civilization: The Middle Colonies.* New York: Charles Scribner's Sons, 1938.

———. *The Old South.* New York: Charles Scribner's Sons, 1942.

Weslager, C.A. *The Log Cabin in America: From Pioneer Days to the Present.* New Brunswick, N.J.: Rutgers University Press, 1969.

White, Edwin E. *Highland Heritage.* New York: Friendship Press, 1937.

Whitwell, W.L. and Lee W. Winborne. *The Architectural Heritage of the Roanoke Valley.* Charlottesville: University Press of Virginia, 1982.

Williams, Samuel Cole, ed. *Early Travels in Tennessee Country, 1540–1800.* Johnson City, Tenn.: Watauga Press, 1928.

Williamson, J.W., ed. *An Appalachian Symposium: Essays Written in Honor of Cratis D. Williams.* Boone, N.C.: Appalachian State University Press, 1977.

Wilson, Eugene H. *Alabama Folk Houses.* Montgomery: Alabama Historical Commission, 1975.

Wilson, Samuel Tyndale. *The Southern Mountaineers.* New York: Presbyterian Home Missions, 1914.

Wynn, Graeme. *Timber Colony: A Historical Geography of Early Nineteenth Century New Brunswick.* Toronto: University of Toronto Press, 1981.

Yoder, Don, ed. *American Folklife.* Austin: University of Texas Press, 1976.
Youngquist, W.G., and Fleischer, H.O. *Wood in American Life, 1776–2076.* Madison, Wisc.: Forest Products Research Society, 1977.
Zelinsky, Wilbur. *The Cultural Geography of the United States.* Englewood Cliffs, N.J.: Prentice-Hall, 1973.

Articles

Amick, H.C. "The Great Valley of East Tennessee." *Economic Geography* 10 (1934):34–52.
Ball, Norman. "Circular Saws and the History of Technology." *Bulletin of the Association for Preservation Technology* 7, no. 3 (1975):79–87.
Barrick, Mac E. "The Log House as Cultural Symbol." *Material Culture* 18, no. 1 (1986):1–26.
Bentley, Blanche. "Tennessee Scotch Irish Ancestry." *Tennessee Historical Magazine* 5, no. 4 (1920):201–211.
Brandt, Lawrence R., and Ned E. Braatz. "Log Buildings in Portage County, Wisconsin: Some Cultural Implications." *Pioneer America* 4, no. 1 (1972):29–39.
Brinkman, Leonard W. "Home Manufacturers as an Indication of an Emerging Appalachian Subculture, 1840-1870." *West Georgia College Studies in the Social Sciences* 12 (1973):50–58.
Buchanan, Paul E. "The Eighteenth-Century Frame Houses of Tidewater, Virginia." In *Building Early America, Contributions Toward the History of a Great Industry,* edited by Peterson, Charles E., 54–73. Radnor, Pa.: Chilton, 1976.
Bucher, Robert C. "The Continental Log House." *Pennsylvania Folklife* 12 (Summer 1962):14–19.
Buckwalter, Donald W. "Effects of Early Nineteenth Century Transportation Disadvantage on the Agriculture of Eastern Tennessee." *Southeastern Geographer* 27 (1987):18–37.
Burnett, Edmund Cody. "Hog Raising and Hog Driving in the Region of the French Broad River." *Agricultural History* 20 (1946):86–103.
———. "Shingle Making on the Lower Waters of the Big Creek of the French Broad River." *Agricultural History* 20 (1946):232–33.
Burns, Inez. "Settlement and Early History of the Coves of Blount County, Tennessee." *East Tennessee Historical Society's Publications* 24 (1952):44–67.

Burt, Jesse C., Jr. "Railroad Promotion of Agriculture in Tennessee." *Tennessee Historical Quarterly* 10 (1951):320–33.
Carroll, Charles F. "The Forest Society of England." In *America's Wooden Age: Aspects of Its Early Technology*, edited by Brooke Hindle, pp. 13–36. Tarrytown, N.Y.: Sleepy Hollow Restorations, 1975.
Chapman, Thomas. "Journal of a Journey through the United States, 1795–96, from the Original Manuscript . . ." *Historical Magazine and Notes and Queries* 15 (June 1869):357–68. Reprinted in *Travels in the Old South*, edited by Eugene L. Schwab, vol. 1, pp. 23–42. Lexington: University Press of Kentucky, 1973.
Clarkson, Roy B. "Mountain Logging in the Appalachians at the Turn of the Century." *Southern Lumberman* 233 (15 Dec. 1976):117–22.
Cobb, P.L. "William Cobb—Host of Gov. Wm. Blount: His Life and Times." *Tennessee Historical Magazine* 9, no. 4 (1928):241–63.
Coffey, Brian. "From Shanty to House: Log Construction in Nineteenth Century Ontario." *Material Culture* 16, no. 2 (1984):61–76.
Connor, Seymour V. "Log Cabins in Texas." *Southwestern Historical Quarterly* 53, no. 2 (1949):105–116.
Conti, Eugene A., Jr. "The Cultural Role of Local Elites in the Kentucky Mountains: A Retrospective Analysis." *Appalachian Journal* 7, nos. 1 and 2 (1979–80):51–68.
Crutchfield, James A. "Pioneer Architecture in Tennessee." *Tennessee Historical Quarterly* 35 (1976):162–74.
DeFriece, Pauline Massengill, and Frank B. Williams, Jr. "Rocky Mount: The Cobb-Massengill Home, First Capitol of the Territory South of the River Ohio." *Tennessee Historical Quarterly* 25 (1966):119–34.
DesChamps, Margaret Burr. "Early Days in the Cumberland Country." *Tennessee Historical Quarterly* 6 (1947):195–229.
DeVivo, Michael S. "The Deforestation of Western North Carolina: 1900–1920." *Pioneer America Society Transactions* 9 (1986):89–94.
Doucet, Michael J., and John C. Weaver. "Material Culture and the North American House: The Era of the Comman Man, 1870–1920." *Journal of American History* 72 (1985):560–87.
Dunn, Durwood. "The Folk Culture of Cades Cove, Tennessee." *Tennessee Folklore Society Bulletin* 43, no. 2 (1977):67–87.
Eller, Ronald D. "Land and Family: An Historical View of Pre-industrial Appalachia." *Appalachian Journal* 6 (Winter 1979):83–109.

Ensminger, Robert F. "A Search for the Origin of the Pennsylvania Barn." *Pennsylvania Folklife* 30 (Winter 1980–81):50–69.

Evans, E. Raymond. "The Strip House in Tennessee Folk-Architecture." *Tennessee Folklore Society Bulletin* 42, no. 5 (1976):163–66.

Field, Walker, Jr. "A Re-Examination into the Invention of the Balloon Frame." *Journal of Society of Architectural Historians* 2 (Oct. 1942): 3–29.

Fielder, George F. "Folk Architecture in Tennessee: A Call for New Directions." *Tennessee Anthropologist* 1, no. 1 (1976):48-57.

Gersmehl, Phil. "Factors Leading to Mountaintop Grazing in the Southern Appalachians." *Southeastern Geographer* 10 (1970):67–72.

Gilman, Fred H. "History of the Development of Sawmill and Woodworking Machinery." *Mississippi Valley Lumberman* 36 (1 Feb. 1895): 59–68.

Glassie, Henry, "The Appalachian Log Cabin." *Mountain Life and Work* 39, no. 4 (1963):5–14.

———. "The Smaller Outbuildings of the Southern Mountains." *Mountain Life and Work* 40, no. 1 (1964):1–6.

———. "The Old Barns of Appalachia." *Mountain Life and Work* 40, no. 2 (1965):21–30.

———. "The Pennsylvania Barn in the South." *Pennsylvania Folklife* 15, no. 2 (Winter 1965–66):8–19.

———. "The Pennsylvania Barn in the South," part 2. *Pennsylvania Folklife* 15, no. 4 (Summer 1966):12–25.

———. "Types of the Southern Mountain Cabin." In *The Study of American Folklore*, edited by Jan H. Brunvand, pp. 338–70. New York: Norton, 1968.

———. "A Central Chimney Continental Log House." *Pennsylvania Folklife* 18 (Winter 1968–69):32–40.

———. "The Double-Crib Barn in South Central Pennsylvania." *Pioneer America* 1, no. 1 (1969):9–16.

———. "The Double-Crib Barn," part 2. *Pioneer America* 1, no. 2 (1969): 40–45.

———. "The Double Crib Barn in South Central Pennsylvania," part 3. *Pioneer America* 2, no. 1 (1970):47–52.

———. "The Double-Crib Barn in South Central Pennsylvania," part 4. *Pioneer America* 2, no. 2 (1970):23–24.

Greve, Jeanette S. "Traditions of Gatlinburg." *East Tennessee Historical Society's Publications* 3 (1931):62–77.

Gritzner, Charles F. "The Scope of Cultural Geography." *Journal of Geography* 65 (1966):4–11.

———. "Log Housing in New Mexico." *Pioneer America* 3, no. 1 (1971): 54–62.

———. "Construction Materials in a Folk Housing Tradition: Considerations Governing Their Selection in New Mexico." *Pioneer America* 6, no. 1 (1974):25–39.

Hart, John Fraser. "Land Rotation in Appalachia." *Geographical Review* 67 (1977):148–66.

Hsiung, David C. "How Isolated Was Appalachia?" *Appalachian Journal* 16 (1989):336–49.

Hulan, Richard H. "Middle Tennessee and the Dogtrot House." *Pioneer America* 7, no. 2 (1975):37–46.

———. "The Dogtrot and its Pennsylvania Associations." *Pennsylvania Folklife* 26 (Summer 1977):25–32.

Hutslar, Donald A. "The Log Architecture of Ohio." *Ohio History* 80 (1971):172–271.

———. "Ohio Waterpowered Sawmills." *Ohio History* 84 (1975):4–56.

Jensen, Robert. "Board and Batten Siding and the Balloon Frame: Their Incompatibility in the Nineteenth Century." *Journal of Society of Architectural Historians* 30 (1971):40–50.

Jordan, Terry G. "The Imprint of the Upper and Lower South on Mid-Nineteenth-Century Texas." *Annals of the Association of American Geographers* 57 (1967):667–90.

———. "The Texas Appalachia." *Annals of the Association of American Geographers* 60 (1970):409–427.

———. "Log Construction in the East Cross Timbers of Texas." *Proceedings of the Pioneer America Society* 2 (1973):107–124.

———. "Log Corner-Timbering in Texas." *Pioneer America* 8, no. 1 (1976): 8–18.

———. "Alpine, Alemannic, and American Architecture." *Annals of the Association of American Geographers* 70 (1980):154–80.

———. "A Reappraisal of Fenno-Scandian Antecedents for Midland American Log Construction." *Geographical Review* 73 (1983):58–94.

———. "Moravian, Schwenkfelder, and American Log Construction." *Pennsylvania Folklife* 33 (Spring 1984):98–124.
Jordan, Terry G., and Matti Kaups. "Folk Architecture in Cultural and Ecological Context." *Geographical Review* 77 (1987):52–75.
Jordan, Terry G., Matti Kaups, and Richard M. Lieffort. "New Evidence on the European Origin of Pennsylvania V Notching." *Pennsylvania Folklife* 36 (Autumn 1986):20–31.
———. "Diamond Notching in America and Europe." *Pennsylvania Folklife* 36 (Winter 1986–87):70–78.
Kauffman, Henry J. "The Pennsylvania Log Barn." In *The Pennsylvania Barn*, edited by Alfred Shoemaker, 23–24. Lancaster: Pennsylvania Dutch Folklore Center, 1955.
Kaups, Matti. "Log Architecture in America: European Antecedents in a Finnish Context." *Journal of Cultural Geography* 2 (1981):131–53.
———. "Finnish Log Houses in the Upper Middle West: 1890–1920." *Journal of Cultural Geography* 3 (1983):2–26.
Kniffen, Fred B. "Louisiana House Types." *Annals of the Association of American Geographers* 26 (1936):179–93.
———. "Geography and the Past." *Journal of Geography* 50 (1951):126–29.
———. "To Know the Land and its People." *Landscape* 9, no. 3 (1960): 20–23.
———. "Folk Housing: Key to Diffusion." *Annals of the Association of American Geographers* 55 (1965):549–77.
———. "On Corner-Timbering." *Pioneer America* 1, no. 1 (1969):1–8.
Kniffen, Fred, and Henry Glassie. "Building in Wood in the Eastern United States: A Time-Place Perspective." *Geographical Review* 56 (1966):40–66.
Lambert, Robert S. "Logging on the Little River, 1890–1940." *East Tennessee Historical Society's Publications* 33 (1961):32–42.
———. "Logging the Great Smokies, 1880–1930." *Tennessee Historical Quarterly* 21 (1961):350–63.
Leuthold, Frank O. "Commuting Patterns of the Tennessee Population." *Tennessee Farm and Home Science*, Progress Report 92 (Oct. 1974), 6–9.
Lewis, Peirce F. "Common Houses, Cultural Spoor." *Landscape* 19, no. 2 (1975):1–22.
———. "The Future of the Past: Our Clouded Vision of Historic Preservation." *Pioneer America* 7, no. 2 (1975):1–20.

———. "Axioms for Reading the Landscape." In *the Interpretation of Ordinary Landscapes*, edited by D.W. Meinig, 11–32. New York: Oxford Univ. Press, 1979.

———. "Defining a Sense of Place." *Southern Quarterly* 17, nos. 3–4 (1979): 24–46.

———. "Learning from Looking: Geographic and Other Writing about the American Cultural Landscape." *American Quarterly* 35, no. 3 (1983):242–61.

Lewis, T.M.N. "Cherokee Log Cabins." *Tennessee Archaeologist* 7, no. 2 (1951):60–61.

Lounsbury, Carl. "The Building Process in Antebellum North Carolina." *North Carolina Historical Review* 60, no. 4 (1983):431–56.

MacClintock, S.S. "The Kentucky Mountains and their Feuds." *American Journal of Sociology* 7, no. 1 (1901):1–28.

McDonald, Forrest, and Grady McWhiney. "The Antebellum Southern Herdsman: A Reinterpretation." *Journal of Southern History* 41 (1975): 147–66.

McKenzie, Adele. "At Brick Mill—Six Generations of Henrys." *Maryville-Alcoa Daily Times*, 24 Feb. 1972.

Marshall, Howard Wight. "The 'Thousand Acres' Log House, Monroe County, Indiana." *Pioneer America* 3, no. 1 (1971):48–56.

Martin, Charles E. "Head of Hollybush: Reconstructing Material Culture Through Oral History." *Pioneer America* 13, no. 1 (1981):3–16.

Medford, Joy. "The Problem of Vernacular Structures in the Historic Preservation Process: Examples from Knox County, Tennessee." In *Proceedings of Conference on Appalachian Geography*, 30–37. Athens, W. Va.: Geography Department, Concord College, 1986.

Messler, Louise Langstrath. "Cloyd's Creek." *Maryville Times*, 8 June 1942.

Meyer, Douglas K. "Diffusion of Upland South Folk Housing to the Shawnee Hills of Southern Illinois." *Pioneer America* 7, no. 2 (1975): 56–66.

Michael, Ronald L. "Cut Nail Manufacture: Southwestern Pennsylvania." *Bulletin of the Association for Preservation Technology* 6, no. 1 (1974):99–100.

Mitchell, Steve, Donald R. Brown, and Michael L. Swanda. "Board Shanty: Box Construction in White County, Arkansas." *Pioneer America Society Transactions* (1987):9–16.

Moffett, Marian, and Lawrence Wodehouse. "The Cantilever Barn in East Tennessee." *Pioneer America Society Transactions* 9 (1986):17–22.

Morgan, John. "An Examination of Log Dwellings in a Cumberland Plateau County of East Tennessee." In *Proceedings of Conference on Appalachian Geography*. 113–25. Athens, W.Va.: Geography Department, Concord College, 1982.

———. "Patterns of House Construction in Rural East Tennessee before 1900." In *Proceedings of Third Conference on Appalachian Geography*, 20–29. Athens, W. Va.: Geography Department, Concord College, 1986.

———. "Difficulty in Obtaining Lumber in Antebellum East Tennessee: Its Impact on House Construction Patterns." In *Proceedings of Fourth Conference on Appalachian Geography*, 23–30. Athens, W. Va.: Geography Department, Concord College, 1988.

Morgan, John, and Ashby Lynch, Jr. "The Log Barns of Blount County, Tennessee." *Tennessee Anthropologist* 9, no. 2 (1984):85–103.

Morgan, John, and Joy Medford. "Log Houses in Grainger County, Tennessee." *Tennessee Anthropologist* 5, no. 2 (1980):137–58.

Nelson, Lee H. "Nail Chronology as an Aid to Dating Old Buildings." *History News* 19, no. 2 (1963). Reprinted as American Association for State and Local History, Technical Leaflet 15.

Nelson, Walter R. "Some Examples of Plank House Construction and their Origin." *Pioneer America* 1, no. 2 (1969):18–29.

Newton, Milton. "Cultural Preadaptation and the Upland South." *Geoscience and Man* 5 (1974):143–54.

Newton, Milton B., Jr., and Linda Pulliam-DiNapoli. "Log Houses as Public Occasions: A Historical Theory." *Annals of the Association of American Geographers* 67 (1977):360–83.

Nichols, William H. "Some Foundations of Economic Development in the Upper East Tennessee Valley, 1850–1900," part 1. *Journal of Political Economy* 64 (1956):277–302.

———. "Some Foundations of Economic Development in the Upper East Tennessee Valley, 1900–1950," part 2. *Journal of Political Economy* 64 (1956):400–415.

———. "Human Resources and Industrial Development in the Upper East Tennessee Valley, 1900–1950." *Quarterly Journal of Economics* 71 (1957):289–316.

O'Malley, James Ross. "Functional Aspects of Folk Housing: A Case for the 'I' House, Union County, Tennessee." *Tennessee Folklore Society Bulletin* 38, no. 1 (1972):1–4.

———. "The 'I' House: An Indicator of Agricultural Attainment in the Southern Appalachian Valley." In *West Virginia and Appalachia: Selected Readings*, edited by Howard G. Adkins, Steve Ewing, and Chester Zimolzak, 105–113. Dubuque, Iowa: Kendall-Hunt, 1977.

O'Malley, James R., and John B. Rehder. "The Two-Story Log House in the Upland South." *Jornal of Popular Culture* 11 (1978):904–915.

Otto, John Solomon. "The Decline of Forest Farming in Southern Appalachia." *Journal of Forest History* 27 (1983):18–27.

Otto, John Solomon, and Nain Estelle Anderson. "The Diffusion of Upland South Folk Culture, 1790–1840." *Southeastern Geographer* 22 (1982):89–98.

Owsley, Frank L. "The Pattern of Migration and Settlement on the Southern Frontier." *Journal of Southern History* 11 (1945):147–76.

Owsley, Frank L., and Harriet C. Owsley. "The Economic Structure of Rural Tennessee, 1850–1860." *Journal of Southern History* 8 (1942): 161–82.

Parker, Russell D. "Alcoa, Tennessee: The Early Years, 1919–1939." *East Tennessee Historical Society's Publications* 48 (1976):84–103.

Peterson, Charles E. "Sawdust Trail." *Bulletin of the Association for Preservation Technology* 5, no. 2 (1973):84–153.

Pillsbury, Richard. "Patterns in the Folk and Vernacular House Forms of the Pennsylvania Culture Region." *Pioneer America* 9, no. 1 (1977): 12–29.

Price, H. Wayne. "The Persistence of a Tradition: Log Architecture in Jersey County, Illinois." *Pioneer America Society Transactions* (1988): 54–62.

Priess, Peter. "Wire Nails in North America." *Bulletin of Association for Preservation Technology* 5, no. 4 (1973):87–92.

Pudup, Mary Beth. "The Boundaries of Class in Preindustrial Appalachia." *Journal of Historical Geography* 15 (1989):139–62.

Pursell, Carroll W., Jr. "The History of Technology and the Study of Material Culture." *American Quarterly* 35 (1983):304–315.

Rehder, John B., John Morgan, and Joy L. Medford. "The Decline of Smokehouses in Grainger County, Tennessee." *West Georgia College Studies in the Social Sciences* 18 (1979):75–83.

Richards, J. "A Treatise on the Construction and Operation of Woodworking Machines." *Forest History* 9, no. 4 (1966):16–23. Excerpt from the original work of the same name, London: E. 2nd F.N. Spon, 1872.

Ritchie, T. "Plankwall Framing, a Modern Wall Construction with an Ancient History." *Journal of Society of Architectural Historians* 30 (1971):66–70.

Roberts, Warren E. "Folk Architecture in Context: The Folk Museum." *Proceedings of the Pioneer America Society* 1 (1972):34–50.

———. "The Tools Used in Building Log Houses in Indiana Houses." *Pioneer America* 9, no. 1 (1977):32–61.

Rogers, William Flinn. "Life in East Tennessee near End of Eighteenth Century." *East Tennessee Historical Society's Publications* 1 (1929): 27–42.

Rosenberg, Nathan. "America's Rise to Woodworking Leadership." In *America's Wooden Age: Aspects of its Early Technology*, edited by Brooke Hindle, 37–62. Tarrytown, N.Y.: Sleepy Hollow Restorations, 1975.

Sauer, Carl. "The Morphology of Landscape." *University of California Publications in Geography* 2, no. 2 (1925):19–54.

Saunders, Thomas I. "Letter from East Tennessee." *United Presbyterian*, March 25, 1880, 202.

Scofield, Edna. "The Evolution and Development of Tennessee Houses." *Journal of the Tennessee Academy of Science* 11, no. 4 (1936):229–40.

Scott, A.E. "A Visit to Mitchell and Roan Mountains." *Appalachia* 4, no. 1 (1884):12–20.

Sprague, Paul E. "The Origin of Balloon Framing." *Journal of the Society of Architectural Historians* 40 (1981):311–19.

Tebbetts, Dianne. "Traditional Houses of Independence County, Arkansas." *Pioneer America* 10, no. 1 (1978):37–55.

Trevena, Billy J., and Lynn J. Garrett. "Industrialization and Part-Time Farming in Upper East Tennessee." *Tennessee Farm and Home Science*, Progress Report 100 (1976), 19–21.

Trindell, Roger T. "Building in Brick in Early America." *Geographical Review* 58 (1968):484–87.

Upton, Dell. "Traditional Timber Framing," In *Material Culture of the Wooden Age*, edited by Brooke Hindle, 35–93. Tarrytown, N.Y.: Sleepy Hollow Press, 1981.

———. "The Power of Things: Recent Studies in American Vernacular Architecture." *American Quarterly* 35 (1983):262–79.

Van Noppen, John, and Ina Woestemeyer Van Noppen. "The Genesis of Forestry in the Southern Appalachians: A Brief History." *Appalachian Journal* 1, no. 1 (1972):63–71.

Vincent, George A. "A Retarded Frontier." *American Journal of Sociology* 4, no. 1 (1898):1–20.

Wacker, Peter O., and Roger T. Trindell. "The Log House in New Jersey: Origins and Diffusion." *Keystone Folklore Quarterly* 13, no. 4 (1968): 248–68.

Walpole, Matthew R. "The Closing of the Open Range in Watauga County, N.C." *Appalachian Journal* 16 (1989):320–35.

Weals, Vic. "It's an Old, Old Road to Warner Martin's Mill." *Knoxville Journal*, 15 Dec. 1977.

———. "Idle Mill Gone with the Wind." *Knoxville Journal*, 29 Dec. 1977.

———. "Cove Lumber Plentiful—Road to Market Steep." *Knoxville Journal*, 7 Jan. 1982.

———. "Strattons Left Name on Mountain." *Knoxville Journal*, 22 Dec. 1983.

———. "Each Member Had a Hand in Building the Stratton Home." *Knoxville Journal*, 29 Dec. 1983.

Weeks, Stephen B. "Tennessee: A Discussion on the Sources of Its Population and the Lines of Immigration." *Tennessee Historical Magazine* 2, no. 4 (1916):245–53.

Weslager, C.A. "Log Houses in Pennsylvania During the Seventeenth Century," *Pennsylvania History* 22 (1955):256–66.

———. "Log Structures in New Sweden During the Seventeenth Century," *Delaware History* 5, no. 2 (1952):77–92.

Wilhelm, Gene, Jr. "Appalachian Isolation: Fact or Fiction?" In *An Appalachian Symposium: Essays in Honor of Cratis D. Williams*, edited by J.W. Williamson, 77–91. Boone, N.C.: Appalachian State University, 1977.

———. "Folk Settlements in the Blue Ridge Mountains." *Appalachian Journal* 5, no. 2 (1978):204–245.

Williams, Michael Ann. "Rethinking the House: Interior Space and Social Change." *Appalachian Journal* 14 (1987):174–87.

Williams, Samuel C. "The Conquest of the Old Southwest." *Tennessee Historical Magazine* 5, no. 4 (1920):212–15.
Willis, Stanley. "Log Houses in Southwest Virginia: Tools Used in Their Construction." *Virginia Cavalcade* 21, no. 4 (1972):36–47.
Wilson, Eugene M. "The Single-Pen Log House in the South," *Pioneer America* 2, no. 1 (1970):21–28.
———. "Some Similarities between American and European Folk Houses," *Pioneer America* 3, no. 3 (1971):8–14.
———. "Form Changes in Folk Houses." *Geoscience and Man* 5 (1974): 65–71.
Wilson, H. Weber. "Basic Timber Framing Exposed." *The Old-House Journal* 5, no. 2 (1977):15–17.
Wolfe, Margaret Ripley. "The Appalachian Reality: Ethnic and Class Diversity," *East Tennessee Historical Society's Publications* 52–53 (1980–81):40–60.
Wright, Martin. "The Antecedent of the Double-Pen House Type," *Annals of the Association of American Geographers* 48 (1958):109–117.
Zelinsky, Wilbur. "The Log House in Georgia." *Geographical Review* 63 (1953):173–93.

Newspapers

Blount County Democrat, Maryville, Tenn., 1882–83.
Brownlow's Knoxville Whig and Independent Journal, 1854–57.
East Tennessean, Maryville, Tenn., 1855–58.
East Tennessee News, Maryville, Tenn., 1883.
Knoxville Journal, 1977–83.
Knoxville Register, 1834–49.
Maryville-Alcoa Daily Times, 1972.
Maryville Index, 1878.
Maryville Record, 1904.
Maryville Times, 1886–1942.
New York Tribune, 1855.
Northwestern Lumberman, Chicago, 1882–94.
The Republican, Maryville, Tenn., 1870–74.
The Watchman, Maryville, Tenn., 1882–83.

Unpublished Manuscripts, Theses, and Dissertations

Baskin, Eugene Haskell. "The Geography of Binfield Community." Master's thesis, University of Tennessee, Knoxville, 1956.

Brewer, George E. "History of Coosa County, Alabama." Manuscript in Alabama Department of Archives and History, Montgomery, Alabama.

Bryan, Charles Faulkner. "The Civil War in East Tennessee: A Social, Political and Economic Study." Ph.D. dissertation, University of Tennessee, Knoxville, 1978.

Burchfield, William V., Jr. "The Unaka Mountains of Tennessee and North Carolina." Master's thesis, University of Tennessee, Knoxville, 1941.

Clendenen, Harbert Leslie. "Settlement Morphology of the Southern Courtois Hills, Missouri, 1820–1860." Ph.D. dissertation, Louisiana State University, Baton Rouge, 1973.

Dunn, Durwood Clay. "Cades Cove During the Nineteenth Century." Ph.D. dissertation, University of Tennessee, Knoxville, 1976.

Gillenwater, Mack H. "Cultural and Historical Geography of Mining Settlements in the Pocahontas Coal Field of Southern West Virginia, 1880 to 1930." Ph.D. dissertation, University of Tennessee, Knoxville, 1972.

Gusler, Mary Ann. "Folk Housing in Patrick County, Virginia." Master's thesis, Arizona State University, 1973.

Historic Buildings Surveys of East Tennessee Counties, including Blount, Grainger, Hamblen, Jefferson, Meigs, Morgan, Unicoi, and Union. Tennessee Historical Commission, Nashville, 1978–84.

Houts, Paul G. "An Education, Economic and Community Survey of Blount County, Tennessee." Master's thesis, University of Tennessee, Knoxville, 1928.

Love, A.H. "The History of Louisville, Blount County, Tennessee." Manuscript written in 1922. In Special Collections, University of Tennessee Library, Knoxville.

Martin, Walter. "Agricultural Commercialism in the Nashville Basin, 1850–1860." Ph.D. dissertation, University of Tennessee, Knoxville, 1984.

Moore, Tyrel Gilce, Jr. "The Role of Ferry Crossings in the Development of the Transportation Network in East Tennessee, 1790–1974." Master's thesis, University of Tennessee, Knoxville, 1975.

———. "An Historical Geography of Economic Development in Appalachian Kentucky, 1800–1930." Ph.D. dissertation, University of Tennessee, Knoxville, 1984.

Nesbitt, William A. "History of Early Settlement and Land Use on the Bent Creek Experimental Forest, Buncombe County, N.C." Report prepared for Appalachian Forest Experiment Station, Asheville, N.C., 1941.

O'Malley, James Ross. "The 'I' House: An Indicator of Agricultural Opulence in Upper East Tennessee." Master's thesis, University of Tennessee, Knoxville, 1972.

Rogers, William Flinn. "Life on the Kentucky-Tennessee Frontier Near the End of the Eighteenth Century." Master's thesis, University of Tennessee, Knoxville, 1925.

U.S. Bureau of the Census. Seventh Census of the United States (1850), Agriculture, Blount County, Tennessee.

———. Seventh Census of the United States (1850), Population, Blount County, Tennessee.

———. Eighth Census of the United States (1860), Agriculture, Blount County, Tennessee.

———. Eighth Census of the United States (1860), Population, Blount County, Tennessee.

———. Ninth Census of the United States (1870), Population, Blount County, Tennessee.

———. Tenth Census of the United States (1880), Agriculture, Blount County, Tennessee.

———. Tenth Census of the United States (1880), Population, Blount County, Tennessee.

Van Benthuysen, Robert N., Jr. "The Sequent Occupance of Tellico Plains, Tennessee." Master's thesis, University of Tennessee, Knoxville, 1951.

Interviews

Gamble, Bessie, Ellejoy, Tenn., April 1984.
Gamble, James T., Knoxville, Tenn., July 1984.
Garrison, Bessie Pickens, Seymour, Tenn., May 1984.
Hall, Shirley, Greenback, Tenn., April 1984.
Lafell, Mrs. W.O., Louisville, Tenn., June 1984.
McKenzie, Adele, Maryville, Tenn., June 1985.

Prater, J.E., Louisville, Tenn., June 1984.
Shields, A. Randolph, Maryville, Tenn., May 1983.
Smith, Ethel Cox, Louisville, Tenn., June 1984.
Smith, Nellie, Maryville, Tenn., June 1985.
White, Mary, Walland, Tenn., November 1982.

Index

Abernethy, Thomas Perkins, 127n
adaptation, 108
Adkins, Howard G., 123n
affluence, 33–34, 62, 111, 133n; see also wealth
agriculture: in Blount County, 75, 79–81, 86; after Civil War, 80; commercial, 3, 72, 75, 79–81, 86, 109, 113; in East Tennessee, 72; fallow-oriented extensive farming, 13; open-range farming, 14; open-range herding, 13; self-sufficient, 113; in Tennessee, 80, 127n; in Upland South, 13; woodsland-adapted, 13
Alabama, 8, 10, 15–16, 17, 76, 113
Alcoa, 63
Alexandria, Ohio, 15
Allegheny community, 56
Allegheny Mountains, 8, 13
Alynwick, 91
Ambrosia, Vincent, xiii
America, eastern, 7
Anderson, Nain Estelle, 13, 120n

antebellum period, 59, 63, 79, 98, 104, 111, 127n
Appalachia, xiii, 3, 13, 64, 87, 129n
Arbogast, Allen, xiii
architecture, 2; folk, xiii; log, 7; pioneer, 33; see also double-pen house; frame construction; frame house; log construction; log house; single-pen house
Arkansas, 8, 10–11, 107
Arnow, Harriette Simpson, 118n
ash, 60
Augusta, Ga., 14

Baker, James, 92
Baker's Creek, 89
Bales, James, and Company, 96
Ball, Donald B., 122n
Ball, Norman, 129n
balloon frame. See balloon frame construction
balloon frame construction: in Alabama, 4; in Blount County, 100–2, 104, 107; and decline of log construction, 109; de-

balloon frame construction
(*continued*)
scription of, 98–99; development of, 99; diffusion of, 98, 109; in East Tennessee, 98–99, 107; in Ohio, 4; origin of, 132n; photo of, 100; in San Francisco, 99; in the South, 99, 109; in Tennessee, 99; in United States, 4, 104, 110; in upstart American towns, 109

barns, 9, 11, 13, 19, 92, 124n

barter system, 74, 127n

beams, 66; *see also* timber frame construction

beans, 73

beech, 60

Beecher and Post, sawmill of, 93

beehives, 74

Bent Creek, 18

Big Creek, 74

Big Gully, 56

Big Springs, 96–97

blacksmith shops, 19

Bledsoe County, 19

Block House, 96

Blount County: agriculture in, 75, 79–81; balloon frame construction in, 98, 102; box construction in, 102–7; brick house construction in, 44–45, 79, 84–85; buildings survey in, 6, 58; during Civil War, 49; construction innovations in, 98, 102, 104, 107; culture of, 58; decline of log construction in, 51, 56–58; difficulty in obtaining sawn lumber in, 62–65, 87; distribution of houses in, 45, 47–48, 50, 52, 55, 57; double-pen houses in, 45–46; economy of, 58, 72–81; farmers and farm laborers in, 79, 81, 85–86, 104; farmhouses in, 102; fences in, 86; frame house construction in, 44–45, 68–69, 79, 81, 84–86, 88, 93, 101–2, 107; frontier houses in, 44–45; historical and geographical pattern of house construction in, 43–58; history of, 6; house builders in, 81–84; I houses in, 45, 47, 54; local demand for lumber in, 95; log house construction in, 20, 25, 30–31, 33, 35, 38, 40–59, 84; lumbering in, 93–97; manufacturing in, 56; map of, 5; newspapers and magazines in, 86, 92, 94; persistence of log house construction in, 59–78; poor people in, 84, 104; railroads in, 80, 94, 96; river transportation in, 80; sawmilling and sawmills in, 87–97; settlement of, 44; shift from log to frame construction in, 49, 79, 87; single-pen houses in, 28; socioeconomic classes in, 86; as study area, 4–6; timber availability in, 59; towns in, 44, 47, 49, 51, 57; villages in, 47, 49, 51, 57; *see*

also Maryville; East Tennessee
Blount County Historic Trust, xiii, 6
Blue Ridge Mountains, 11, 13, 18, 42
board-and-batten siding, 103–6; photo of, 103; *see also* box construction
board roof, 28–29, 64; photo of, 28; *see also* roofs
Boorstin, Daniel J., 109, 132n–33n
Bourbon County, 15
box construction: in Blount County, 102–3, 107; and decline of log construction, 98, 102, 105, 109; and demise of log construction, 107; description of, 102–3, 106–7; diffusion of, 110; photo of, 103; in the South, 109; in United States, 110; in White County, Arkansas, 133n
box house: abandonment of, 104; in Appalachia, 104, 109; in Arkansas, 109, 133n; in Blount County, 103–5; diffusion of, 110; with double-layer walls, 106–7; insulation capability of, 106; in mining and timber settlements, 110; modification of, 104; photo of, 103; and poor people, 104; social status of, 105; in Upland South, 110; in upper East Tennessee, 106; and yeomen farmers, 104
Boyd, Perry, 97

braced-frame construction, 65, 126n; *see also* timber frame construction
braces, 65, 66, 69; *see also* timber frame construction
Braden, J.W., 93
Brakebill, Peter, house of, 68–69
Brewer, George E., 60, 124n
brick house, 3, 15, 44–45, 76, 79, 84–85; photo of, 47
Brick Mill, 71, 85, 89, 105
Brickey, Peter, house of, 64
Bright, Eddie, xiii
Brinkman, Leonard W., v, xiv
British, 10, 28, 31
British Isles, 7
Brown, Donald R., 132n–33n
Brownlow's, 127n, 130n
Brunvand, Jan H., 117n
Buchanan, Paul E., 126n
Buckwalter, Donald W., 72, 127n–28n
building, house. *See* ballon frame construction; box construction; frame construction; log construction; timber frame construction
building, self-sufficient techniques of, 112
Buncombe County, N.C., 18
Burnett, Edmund Cody, 74, 127n–28n
Burns, Aaron, 78
Burns, Inez E., 6, 64, 119n. 123n, 125n, 128n–31n
Burns, Richard, 78
butter, 73–74

cabbage, 73
Cable, Peter, 78
Cable sawmill, 131n
Cades Cove, 6
Cades Cove: agricultural economy in, 80; carpenters in, 69; farmers in, 97; history of, 6; house building in, 92–93, 96; house destruction in, 5–6; life in, 75; log structures in, 6, 65–66, 112; lumbering in, 92–93, 96–97; outbuildings in, 65; photo of log house in, 66; sawmilling and sawmills in, 92–93, 96–97, 112; social status associated with log houses in, 112
Cades Cove Story, 6
Campbell, John C., 18, 121n
Cape Fear River, 16
capital, 13, 72
capitol, of Territory of Tennessee, 84
Carnes, Linda, 67, 126n
carpenters, 61–62, 69–72, 93, 98, 124n
carpentry, 8, 14, 66, 69, 98, 107, 109
cash crop, lumber as, 96
Cavender, Anthony P., 122n
census manuscripts, 71, 77–78, 81–83, 113
central-chimney house. *See* saddlebag house
change agent, 85
Cheoah, 92
cherry, 60

chestnut, 60, 91
Chestnut Flats, 97
Chicago, 99
chickens, 73–74
Chilhowee, 71
Chilhowee Mountain, 49, 53, 57
chimneys, 22–24, 26, 30, 32, 69, 106; photos of, 26–27
chink construction, 8, 10, 23; *see also* log construction
chinking, 62
Christman, Henry M., 121n
churches, 19
Civil War, 44, 49; conditions after, 16, 18–19, 27, 34, 49, 60, 85, 87, 90, 94, 98–99, 102, 107, 109–10, 112, 115; conditions before, 3, 45, 47–48, 51, 62–63, 68–70, 75–76, 79–81, 85–86, 98, 100, 104
clapboard, 104; *see also* siding
Clark, Blanche Henry, 72, 127n
Clark, Thomas, 78
Clarkson, Roy B., 125n
Cliff community, 56, 96
Clinch Mountain, 35
Clover Hill, 56, 71
Cloyd's Creek, 63, 91
coal mining, 111
coastal plain, 113
Cobb-Massengill house, 84
Cocke County, Tenn., 74
coffee, 74
colonies: American, 7; Middle Atlantic, 28; South Atlantic, 8
commercial lumbering: in Blount County, 87, 93–96; in

Cades Cove, 131n; as cash crop, 96; and decline of log construction, 93; in Ellejoy area, 95; and local demand, 95, 111; and lumber hauling, 94; and lumberyards, 94; as response to outside demand, 94, 111; rise of, 94, 98; and rise of frame construction, 93, 96; role of portable sawmill in, 95, 96, 111; role of railroads in, 94; in Tellico Plains, 110
Condit, Carl W., 126n, 132n
Congaree River, 17
construction. *See* box construction; frame construction; log construction; timber frame construction
construction innovations, 98–107; *see also* balloon frame construction; box construction
convergence, cultural, 114
Coosa County, Ala., 61
corn, 72–74, 79, 127n
corncribs, 17, 19; *see also* outbuildings
corner notches: diffusion of, 11, 13, 42; in East Tennessee, 35–36, 42; in eastern United States, 11–12, 36; geographic pattern of, 11, 13, 42, 108; selection of, 36, 41–42, sketches of, 12; types of, 11–13, 34–36
cotton, 73–74
courthouses, 19
coves, 57

Cox house, 92
Coyte, 71
credit, 74
crops, 79; *see also* agriculture
Crutchfield, James A., 33, 108, 122n–23n
cultural landscape, xiii, 1, 115
culture, 2
culture area, 8; Midland, 8; Upland South, 8
Cumberland house, 31–33; photo of, 32
Curtis, Bill, 92
Cyganiak, Neal, xiii

Danforth, Josiah, sawmill of, 63
Danville, Va., 16
Davis, Cal, 96
Davis, Crof, 92
Davis house, photo of, 27
DeArmond, Milford, 124n
decline, of log house construction: in Blount County, 51, 56–58; construction innovations and, 98–107; sawmilling and lumbering and, 87–97; socioeconomic factors and, 79–86
DeFriece, Pauline Massengill, 128n
DeHart, Jennifer, xiii
Delaware Indians, 14
Delaware Valley, 7, 10
Dennett, John Richard, 16–17, 118n, 121n
DeVivo, Michael, xiv
diamond notch, 8, 13

Dickenson County, Va., 3
diffusion: of balloon construction, 99, 107, 109; of box construction, 110; of corner notches, 11, 13, 42, hierarchical, 109; of log construction, 1, 10–11, 31, 42; of portable circular sawmill, 93, 111
doctrine of first effective settlement, 10, 120n
dogtrot house: in Alabama, 16–17, 32; in Blount County, 33, 46; construction of, 31, 33; diffusion of, 31; in East Tennessee, 31, 33, 108; form of, 31–33; origin of, 9; photos of, 32, 46; in Tennessee, 33
doors, 24, 103
double-box construction, 106; see also box construction
double-pen house, 10, 30–31, 33–34, 45–46, 108; photos of, 31–32, 46; see also Cumberland house; dogtrot house; saddlebag house
droving, 76
Dry Creek, 95
ducks, 73
Duncan, Alexander, 78
Dunn, Durwood, 6, 80, 119n, 128n, 131n
Dutch, 7
Dykeman, Wilma, 128n

East Tennessean, 124n, 126n, 130n

East Tennesseans, 113; see also East Tennessee
East Tennessee: agriculture in, 72–74, 79; barter system in, 74, 127n; buildings surveys in, xiii, 2, 20; carpenters in, 69; chimneys in, 23; chink construction in, 23; Civil War in, 19; corner notches in, 36, 42; cultural history of log house in, 1; double-pen log houses in, 19, 30, 33–34; frame construction in, 65–66, 98, 107, 118n; frontier buildings in, 19; frontier life and economy in, 127n; frontier period in, 72; grasses in 72; history of, 6; landscape of, 115; log buildings in, 19, 122n; log construction in, 1, 16, 19–42, 108, 118n; log house in, 1–2; map of, 21; mountains in, 72; nails in, 70, 72; neighborhood stores in, 74; notch types in, 11, 13; as part of Upland South, 1, 19; single-pen log houses in, 20, 22–23, 25, 30; timber in, 34, 72; traditional economy of, 72–73; types of log houses in, 20; 103; valleys of, 72; vertical plank wall construction in, 103; whip sawing in, 64; see also Blount County
Eastern Seaboard, 126n
economy, 2, 13; agricultural, 3, 109, 113; self-sufficient, 74,

77; traditional, 72–78; see also agriculture
editors, newspaper, 85, 92
eggs, 74
Eighth Census of the United States, 63, 77–78
Ellejoy, 56, 71, 92–93, 131n
Ellejoy Creek, 95
Eller, Ronald D, 3, 87, 109–10, 118n, 128n–32n
Embree, Elihu, 70
Embree, Elijah, 70
Embree's Nails, 70
England, 17, 88; see also English
English, 7, 13, 28, 119n; see also England
Enslow, Ella, 106, 132n–33n
ethnic groups, 7
ethnic mixing, 14
ethnicity, 36
Europe, 8, 103
Evans, E. Raymond, 132n
Everett, Robt., 78
Ewing, Steve, 123n
exchange, 127n

farmers, 34, 69, 79–80, 86, 97; sharecroppers, 72; small, 72–73, 105–6; tenant, 81; valley, 76; yeomen, 72, 76–77, 85, 97, 104; see also agriculture
farmhouses, 1, 102
farming. See agriculture
farms, 72, 75; see also agriculture
fashion, current, 2

Fayetteville, 16
feathers, 74
Feezell, W.M., 93
fences, 17, 51, 86
Field, Walker, Jr., 132n
Finland, 9, 31; see also Finnish; Finns
Finnish, 8; see also Finland; Finns
Finns, 6, 10, 13–14; see also Finland; Finnish
floors, 23, 101
forests: hardwood, 13, 36; pine, 13; softwood, 36
forts, 19
foundations, 23
Fox, Thomas, xiv
frame construction, 3, 65, 101, 112, 114; of houses, 3, 44–45, 53, 57–58, 66, 76, 79, 81, 84–86, 92–93, 109, 112; see also balloon frame construction; timber frame construction
frame house, 3, 4, 15–16, 86, 112, 114; in Alabama, 16; in Blount County, 44–45, 66, 79; construction of, 65–72, 99–102; in East Tennessee, 59; on frontier, 15; see also balloon frame construction; frame construction; timber frame construction
Freedom, Gary, xiv
Freeman, Thomas H., 128n
French Broad River, 128n
Friendsville, 47, 56, 71, 96
frontier, 84; economy of, 127n;

frontier (continued)
  houses of, 44–45; life on, 127n towns, of, 15; see also frontier period
frontier period, 14, 72; see also frontier
frontiersmen, 13–14; see also frontier
fruits, 74
full-dovetail notch, 8, 11–13; sketches of, 12
fusion, of architectural forms, 30

gables, 22, 23, 30–32
Gaddis, M.B., 94
Gallatin, Tenn., 15
Gallipolis, Ohio, 15
Gamble, Hugh, 92
Gamble, James T., 57–58, 124n
Gamble, Josiah, 78
Gamble's Store, 56, 71
Garner, Eli, 78
Garrison, Bessie Pickens, 92, 130n
geese, 73
geographers, cultural, 2
George, J.S., 77
Georgia, 8, 10, 115
German, 9; see also Germans
Germans, 7, 9, 11, 13; see also German
Giedion, Sigfried, 132n
Gilman Fred H., 124n–25n
Glassie, Henry, 12, 20, 26, 28, 30, 42, 108, 117n–20n, 122n
Gold Rush, 99
Grainger County, 19, 24, 26, 28–31, 35–37, 41–42; photos of log structures in, 22, 24, 26, 28, 32, 37
grasses, 72
Gray, Lewis Cecil, 76, 128n
Great Smoky Mountains National Park, 4, 5
Greenback, 91, 96
Greeneville, Tenn., 15
Grindstaff, James, 78
gristmills, 19, 62, 68
Gritzner, Charles F., xiii
grooved-post construction, 103
Guffey, Stan, xiii

half-dovetail notch, 12–13, 36–37, 41–42; photo of, 37; sketches of, 12
half notch, 8, 13
half-timber construction, 119n, 125n–26n
Hall, Shirley, 133n
Hamblen County, 20, 36
Hammond, Edwin H., xiv
hardwoods, 13, 36, 41; see also forests
Hart, John Fraser, 2, 118n
Hatcher, Elijah, 78; house of, 65
Hawkins, A.W., 124n
Hawkins County, 106
hay, 74
Hazel Creek Valley, N.C., 18
Headrick, Daniel, 78
hearth: backcountry, 14; cultural, 120n; Middle Atlantic, 8
heavy frame construction, 119n; see also timber frame construction

Henry, James, 85; sawmill of, 91
Henry, Thomas R., 121n
herding. *See* agriculture
heritage, settlement, 1
hewing, 8, 23, 25, 36, 41, 60, 65, 68–69, 106; *see also* log construction
Hickman, Nollie, 125n
hickory, 60
Hindle, Brooke, 126n, 129n
historic lumpiness, concept of, 114
history, cultural, 1
History of Blount County, 6
Hitch, Archibald, 78
"hollow folk," 18
Holston College, 91
Holston River, 127n
horses, 73
hotels, 19
house builders, 111; characteristics of, 81–84
house construction; *See* balloon frame construction; box construction; frame construction; log construction; timber frame construction
house raising, 60–61
housing: folk, 120n; traditional, 2
Huffstetlers community, 56
Hughes, Thomas, 122n
Hulan, Richard H., 123n
Huntsville, Ala., 70
huts: Indian wigwam, 119n; log, 16–17
Hutslar, Donald A., 3–4, 109, 111–12, 117n–19n, 125n

I house, 34, 45, 47, 54, 123n; photos of, 47, 54
Illinois, 8, 10, 34
Imlay, Gilbert, 14, 121n
Indiana, 8, 10, 34
individualism, 14
industrialization, 129n; *see also* "New South"
innovations. *See* construction innovations
intermarriage, 14
Iowa, 34

Jackson, Jeff, 96
Jackson County, Ala.: photo of house in, 32
jails, 19
Jamestown, 119n
Jefferson County, 20, 36
Jensen, Robert, 132n
Johnson, Elkanah, sawmill of, 91
Johnson, Meade Milton, 130n
Johnson County, 106
joinery, 99; *see also* timber frame construction
joists, 68
Jollie, R.T., xiii
Jonesboro, 15
Jordan, Terry G., xiv, 2, 8–10, 13, 26, 28, 30, 36, 41, 84, 108, 113–14, 117n–20n, 122n–23n, 128n, 133n
journals, travel, 6
Jumper, Sidney, xiv

Kaups, Matti, 8, 13, 117n, 119n–20n, 122n–23n

168 ■ Index

Kennedy, Andrew, sawmill of, 63
Kenner Bros., sawmill of, 92
Kentucky, 8, 10, 14, 18
Kephart, Horace, 121n
kerf, 90
Kerr, Jesse, Jr., 90
Kerr, Maclin, photo of house of, 47
Killebrew, J.B., 19, 51, 60, 85, 88, 90, 118n, 122n–24n, 128n–30n
King, Robert, 70
Kingston, Tenn., 15
Kirby, Richard, 77
kitchens, 17; detached, 25–26; photo of, 66
Kline, Gerald W., 67, 126n
Kniffen, Fred, xiii, 2, 11–12, 36, 42, 117n–20n, 123n
Knox County, 19, 51
Knoxville: carpenters in, 15; confluence of Holston and French Broad rivers, 128n; early houses of, 15; influence on Blount County, 48; market for Blount County agriculture, 75; nails in, 70–71; newspapers of, 90; rail connection with Maryville, 80; recipient of Blount County lumber, 96; as urban center of mid-East Tennessee, 48
Knoxville and Augusta Railroad, 96, 130n
Knoxville and Charleston Railroad, 94, 130n
Knoxville Iron Company, 90

Knoxville Journal, 56
Knoxville Register, 70, 126n–27n
Knoxville Southern Railroad, 95, 96

labor, 13, 60
laborers, farm, 73, 81
Laffell, Mrs. W.O., 91, 130n
Lambert, Robert S., 129n–31n
Lancaster, Pa., 14,
land: agricultural, 49, 79; marginal, 73; public, 73; *see also* agriculture
landlords, 73, 105
Lane, Cal, house of, 124n
Lane, Dr. Sam, 78, 105
Lane and Bodley, 89
Lattimore, Buck, 85
Laurel Creek, 93
Lenoir, William B., 125n
Leuthold, Frank, xiv
Lewis, Peirce F., 2, 114, 118n, 131n, 133n
Lexington, Ky., 15
Little River, 45, 51, 63, 75, 94–95
Little River Lumber Company, 95–97
Little River Railroad, 131n
Little Tennessee River, 128n
livestock, 73; droving of, 76; grazing of, 72, 76; production of, 76, 79–80
locust, 60
log architecture, 7; *see also* log construction; log house
log cabin myth, 119n
log construction: in Blount

Index ■ 169

County, 43–58; decline of, 79–107; in Deleware Valley, 7; diffusion of, 1, 10–11, 31, 42; in early American colonies, 7; in East Tennessee, 1–2, 19–42; in eastern America, 7; Finnish contribution to, 7–10; Germans and, 7, 9–10; of houses, 1–4, 18–86, 112; in Kentucky, 14; Midland influence on, 7–14; in New Sweden, 7; in Northern Europe, 8; in Ohio, 111; in Pennsylvania, 7–8, 111; persistence of, 59–78; in the South, 15; Swedish contributions to, 7–10; in Texas, 2, 84; tradition of, 1; in Upland South, 8, 14, 19; see also log house; Midland log construction

log dwelling. See log house

log house: abandonment of, 109; in Alabama, 4, 16; in Appalachia, 3; in Bledsoe County, 19; in Blount County, 43–58, 85; in Blue Ridge Mountains, 18; builders of, 81–84; in Carolinas, 14; in Congaree River area, in Danville, Virginia area, 16; 17; decline of, 79–107; destruction of, 44; diffusion from Midland area, 11; dominance of, 16–17, 47, 114; in East Tennessee, 1–2, 16, 19–42; enlargement of, 84; form of, 108; in frontier settlements, 15; in Georgia, 3; in Kentucky, 14; in Knox County, 19; in Marion, South Carolina area, 17; in Mississippi, 15; in North Carolina, 16; in Ohio, 14; in Pennsylvania, 10, 14; persistence of, 59–78; in Piedmont, 16; social stigma associated with, 2, 85, 105; in southwestern Virginia, 16; in Tennessee, 14, 20; in Tennessee River Valley, 17; in Upland South, 18 See also log construction

log housing. See log construction; log house

log pen. See pen

logs, floating of, 95

Lohman, Beth, xiii

Looson, Daniel, 78

Loudon County, 91, 96

Louisville, Ky., 18

Louisville, Tenn.: destruction of early houses in 47; as economic center of Blount County, 75; economic disaster in, 80; house construction in, 45, 53; impact of railroad construction on, 81; as port on Tennessee River, 80–81, 128n; railroad construction through, 80, 96; steamboat navigation to, 75;

Lounsbury, Carl, 2, 112–13, 118n

Love, A.H., 80, 128n

lumber, 127n, 131n; access to, 77, 112; entrepreneurs and, 97;

lumber (continued)
    hauling of, 94; see also commercial lumbering
lumbering. See commercial lumbering
lumberyards, 94; see also commercial lumbering
Lynch, Ashby, Jr., xiii, 122n

McClanahan, R.A., 95
McClanahan, Robert, sawmill of, 91
McConnell, Alfred, 78
McConnell, James Campbell, 85
McConnell, Newton, 78
McCullough, Thos., 77
McGill, John, sawmill of, 93
McKenzie, Adele, xiv, 119n, 129n
McKinney, Lynn, xiv
McMahan, M.B., II, 131n–33n
McNutt, Alex., 77
McNutt, James, sawmill of, 63
Madisonville, 92
magazines, 6, 86
mail delivery, 86
mansion-house, 16
manufacturing, 56, 73
Marion, S.C., 17
markets, 72, 113
Martin, Charles E., 106, 133n
Martin, Sally, 77
Martin, "Snakey" John, 124n
Martin, Walter, xiii
Maryland, 10–11
Maryville, 53, 70–71, 91, 94; building boom in, 53, 94; in Civil War, 44; coffin factory in, 131n; as county seat, 47, 95; demand for lumber in, 95; destruction of frame houses in, 44, 47; house construction in, 47, 51, 56; lumberyards in, 94; manufacturing in, 95; newspapers in, 94; residences in, 102; role of railroads in, 94; see also Blount County
Maryville Index, 129n–30n
Maryville Record, 93, 130n
Maryville Republican, 74, 89
Maryville Times, 56, 92, 94–95, 124n, 129n–31n
Massengill, William Allen, 85
Mayfield, Michael, xiii
Mead, H. G., sawmill of, 91
Meadow, 85, 96
Medford, Joy L., xiii-iv, 42, 122n–23n
Meigs County, 20, 36
melting pot, 7
Mercer, Henry C., 125n–26n
Messler, Louise Lanstrath, 125n
Michaux, F.A., 14–15, 121n
Middle Atlantic core. See Middle Atlantic hearth
Middle Atlantic hearth, 8
Middle Tennessee, 15, 31, 72, 75
Midland log construction, 7–18
Midwest, 94, 99
Miller Cove, 53
mills, neighborhood, 110
Milsaps, Jesse, 78
Miser Station, 56, 71
Mississippi, 8, 10, 15
Missouri, 8, 10

Mitchell, Steve, 132n–33n
Monroe County, 64–65
Montell, William Lynwood, 117n–18n
Montvale Springs, 71
Moore, Tyrel, xiv
Morgan, John, 42, 122n–23n
Morgan County, 20, 28–31, 35–36, 39, 41–42; photos of log structures in, 23, 39
Morganton, 71
Morris, Eastin, 15, 70, 121n, 126n
Morse, Michael Lynn, 117n–18n
mortises, 66, 68–69; see also timber frame construction
mountains, 60, 72
mules, 73
Myers, George, 93

nails, 65, 68, 70–72, 102, 126n
Nails Creek, 62, 68
Nashville, 15, 18, 130n
Nashville and Chattanooga Railroad, 76
negroes, 16–17
Nelson, Lee H., 126n
Nelson, Walter R., 132n
Nesbitt, William A., 121n
Neubert, Yank, 97
New England, 10, 103
New Jersey, 10
New Mexico, xiii
New Orleans, 76
"New South," 129n
New Sweden, 7
New World, 17

New York, 16
Newbert, J.G., 92
newspapers, 6, 43, 53, 56, 60, 86, 90–95; advertisements in, 70, 74, 86, 89–90, 127n
Newton, Milton B., Jr., 8, 14, 41, 117n, 119n, 123n
nineteenth century, 1, 3, 5, 14, 59, 61, 65, 78–79, 84, 109, 111
Ninth Census of the United States, 71, 81–82, 87
nogging, 126n
North Carolina, xiii, 8, 10, 13, 16, 33, 42, 44, 105, 113,
Northwestern Lumberman, 129n
notch types. See corner notches
notching. See corner notches
Notime community, 56

O'Malley, James R., 122n–23n
oak, 34–35, 41, 60
oats, 72–73, 79
oblong pen, 108; see also single-pen house; rectangular pen; square pen
Ohio, 8, 10, 111
Ohio River, 15
Oklahoma, 8, 10
Oliver, Elijah, 65, 78; photo of house of, 66
Oliver, John, 78
Oliver, John W., 125n
Olmsted, Frederick Law, 15–16, 121n
onions, 73
opulence, agricultural, 47; see also affluence; wealth

orchards, 74
Otto, John Solomon, 13, 120n
outbuildings, 11, 13, 17, 19, 65
Owsley, Frank L., 73, 124n, 127n
Owsley, Harriet, 73, 127n
oxen, 92

Pace, Robert A., 67, 126n
paneling, 66, 69
Paris, Ky., 15
Patrick, James, 69, 99, 121n–22n, 126n, 130n, 132n
Patty, W.J., 93
peafowls, 73–74
peas, 73
Peery, Ira, house of, 68–69
pegs, 66, 68–69; see also timber frame construction
pen, 26–33, 60–62, 66, 108; see also double-pen house; single-pen house
pen tradition, 30; see also pen
Pennsylvania, 7–11, 13–14, 16, 111, 115
persistence, of log construction: in Blount County, 59–78; difficulty in obtaining sawn lumber and, 62–65; economy and ease of log construction and, 60–62; frame construction before 1860 and, 65–72; timber availability and, 59–60; traditional economy and, 72–78
Peterson, Charles E., 125n–26n
Pickens, Robert, 77
Pickens, Samuel L., 92

Piedmont, 16, 76, 113
piers, 23
Pigeon Forge Park, 67
Pillsbury, Richard, 3, 111–12, 115, 118n, 133n
pine, 13, 34–35, 41, 60, 91
pioneer period, 1, 85
pioneers, 11
Pistol Creek, 63
plank house, 105; see also box house
plantations, 17–18, 76
planters, 17
plates, 65, 68–69, 103
poor people, 34, 77, 84, 104, 133n
"poor white trash," 17
"poor whites," 15
poplar, 34–35, 41, 60
porches, 24
Porter, Jas., 77
Porter, Stephen S., 77
post-and-beam construction, 65; see also timber-frame construction
post offices, 71
posts, 65–66, 68–69, 102
potatoes, 73
Powell, C., 70
Powell, T.J., 70
Prater, "Buffalo" Jim, 91, 104
Prater, J.E., 53, 57–58, 91, 104, 123n–24n, 130n–31n, 133n
preadaptive traits, 14
Proceedings of Conference on Appalachian Geography, xiv

Pulliam-DiNapoli, Linda, 41, 117n, 123n
puncheons, 64

rafters, 25, 61; see also roofs
railroads, 76, 80, 96–97, 111, 113, 130n
rectangular pen, 26, 28, 108; see also pen; single-pen house
Reed, Asbury, 97
Rehder, John B., xiii, 122n
renters, 73
Richards, J., 89, 129n–30n
ridgepole-and-purlin roof, 8, 24, 65–66; see also roofs
Riedl, Norbert F., 122n
Ritchie, T., 132n
river transportation, 75–76, 80
Riverside, 97; see also Walland
Roberts, Lisa, xiv
Roberts, Warren E., 36, 41, 123n
Robinson, Solon, 99–102, 132n
Rockford, 45, 47, 49, 71, 91, 94–95
Rocky Branch, 61
Rogers, Asa, 78
Rogers, Steve, xiii
Rogers, William Flinn, 127n
roofs, 8–9, 24–25, 28–29, 61, 64–66
Rosenberg, Nathan, 129n
Roth, Leland M., 132n
Rowntree, Lester, 8
rural elite, 85
rural society, 86

saddle notch, 8, 11–13, 36, 41–42; photo of, 39; sketches of, 12

saddlebag house, 30–31, 33, 108; see also double-pen house
salt, 74
San Francisco, 99
Saunders, Thomas I., 51, 58, 74, 80, 123n, 127n–28n
sawmilling, 87–88, 93, 98, 109; custom, 63, 93, 95, 131; see also commercial lumbering; sawmills
sawmills: access to, 3, 64, 76, 87, 112; in Appalachia, 3, 63, 87; in Blount County, 46, 62, 88–91, 94–95, 110; in Cades Cove, 93; circular, 88–89; and commercial lumbering, 93; and custom milling, 93; and decline of log construction, 3, 87, 109–10; in East Tennessee, 62, 88, 90; in Ellejoy area, 95; impact of portable mill on housebuilding, 92–93; portable, 88–89, 92–93, 96; and rise of frame construction, 87–88; sales of, 89; sash, 46, 88; in Sevier County, 97; steam-powered, 89–90; in Sweetwater Valley, 64; in Tellico Plains, 110; transfer of, 91–92, 96; in United States, 88; water-powered, 46, 88, 91, 93; see also commercial lumbering; sawmilling
saws: circular, 88–89; pit, 64, 125n; rip, 64; sash, 63; up-and-down, 63; whip, 64–65; see also sawmills

Sawyer's Creek, 92
Scandinavia, 103
schools, 19
Scofield, Edna, 33, 108, 122n–23n
Scotch-Irish, 7, 11, 13, 28
Scott, A.E., 105, 132n–33n
Seaton community, 56
semilunate notch, 36
Sequatchie County, 85
servant cabins, 17
settlement, 47; of Blount County, 44; Midland in Upland South, 13–14; mining, 110; nucleated, 15, 57; scattered pattern of, 14; timber 110
Sevier County, 19, 67–68, 91, 97, 105
shaping of logs, 23, 41; see also log construction
sharecroppers, 72; see also farmers
Shaw, Samuel, sawmill of, 63
Shenandoah Valley, 11
Sherman, Mandel, 18, 121n
Shields, A. Randolph, 6, 75, 119n, 124n, 127n–28n, 130n
shifting cultivation, 14
shingle makers, 74
shingled roof, 9; see also roofs
shingles, 74
shipping business, 81
Shooks Gap, Tenn., 92
Shurtleff, Harold R., 117n, 119n
siding, 64, 84–85, 103–7, 126n
sills, 68–69, 101–3
simplification, of log construction, 42

single-pen house, 9–11; chimneys of, 23–24; construction of, 20, 23–25; description of, 10–11, 20; doors of, 24; enlargement of, 25, 30–31, 33; floors of, 23; foundation of, 23; piers and, 23; photos of, 22–24, 26; roof construction on, 24–25; shaping of logs on, 23; types of, 20, 26, 28, 30; wall construction of, 23; windows of, 24; see also rectangular pen; square pen
sleepers, 100, 102
Smith, Ethel Cox, 130n; house of, 91
Smith, Nellie, 130n–31n
smokehouses, 17, 19; see also outbuildings
snake fence, 17; see also fences
social status, 84, 106
social stigma, 84, 86, 109, 113, 114
socioeconomic classes, 86
socioeconomic factors: and decline of log house construction, 79–86
softwoods, 36, 41; see also forests
soils, 72
Somers, Robert, 17–18, 118n, 121n
sorghum, 73
South, 15–16, 42, 16, 99, 109–10
South Carolina, 8, 10
Southern Highlands, 18
southern mountains, 30

Sparks, Howard, 97, 131n
Sparks, J.T., 93
Sparks, S.L., sawmill of, 93
spinning wheel, 75
splash dams, 95
Sprague, Paul E., 132n
square notch, 12–13, 87; photo of, 40; sketches of, 12
square pen, 26, 28, 108; see also single-pen house
squatters, 73
stable, 17
"starter" houses, 84
steamboat business, 81
steam engines, 90; see also sawmills
steam power, 88; see also sawmills
steam wagons, 92; see also sawmills
Steila, Donald, xiii
stone houses, 44–45, 84
stores, 19, 74
Stratton, John, 65
studs, 65–66, 69, 103
sugar, 74
surveys, building, xiii, 2, 6, 19–20, 28–35, 43, 53, 58, 106, 122n
Swanda, Michael L., 132n–33n
Sweden, 9; see also Swedes; Swedish
Swedes, 7, 10, 13, 28; see also Sweden; Swedish
Swedish, 8; see also Sweden; Swedes
sweet gum, 60

Sweetwater, Tenn., 64
Sweetwater Valley, 64

taverns, 19
taxes, 74
Taylor, Dr. Andrew Jackson, house of, 102
Tebbetts, Diane, 132n
Tellico Plains, 110
tenants, 72, 81, 133n; see also farmers
Tennessee, 69, 99, 107; agriculture in, 127n; architectural resources in, 6; buildings survey in, 6; dogtrot house in, 33; as part of Upland South, 8; pioneer architecture in, 33; as recipient of Midland log construction, 10, 13; Territory of, 84; wheat in, 76; see also East Tennessee
Tennessee Anthropologist, xiv
Tennessee Gazeteer, 70
Tennessee Historical Commission, xiii, 6, 122n
Tennessee River, 45, 80, 75, 128n
Tennessee River Valley, 17; see also Tennessee River; Tennessee Valley
Tennessee Valley, 76; see also Tennessee River; Tennessee Valley
Tennessee Valley Authority, 122n
tenons, 66, 68, 69; see also timber frame construction
Tenth Census of the United States, 87, 90–91

Territory of Tennessee, 84; see also Tennessee
Texas, 2, 8, 10, 26, 30, 36, 84, 113–14
Thompson-Brown house, photos of, 38, 46
Thwaites, Reuben Gold, 121n
Tidewater South, 10
timber: availability of, 59–60; in East Tennessee, 34–35, 72; and selection of corner notches, 36, 41; types of, 34–36, 41; see also oak; pine; poplar
timber frame construction: in Blount County, 66, 68–69, 102, 107; description of, 66, 69; development of, 125n; in East Tennessee, 65–66; sketch of, 67; in Tennessee, 126n; in United States, 3
Tipton, Jacob, 78
tobacco, 73–74
Toole's Hardware, Maryville, Tenn., 70
topographic maps, 6
topography, 72
towns, 15, 44, 49, 56
Townsend, 96, 131n
tradition, cultural, 36, 42, 108
transportation, 72, 75–76, 92
tree species, 34; see also timber
trusses, 69
Tuckaleechee Cove, 69, 71
Turner, Frederick Jackson, 8, 119n
twentieth century, 1, 18, 112

Unicoi County, 20, 36
Union County, 20, 31, 35–36, photo of house in, 31
United States, 1, 9, 11–12, 14, 36, 88, 104, 110, 125n–26n
United States Bureau of Census, 125n–26n, 129n
United States Census of Agriculture, 79, 128n
United States Department of Agriculture, 122n
Unitia, 71
Upland South: agriculture in, 13; barns and outbuildings in, 11; box houses in, 110; as culture area, 8; delimitation of, 8; forests of, 13; I houses in, 34, 47; landscape of, xiii; mining and timber settlements in, 110; regional housing patterns in, 18; sawmills in, 62; settlement of, 13–14; single-pen house in, 30
Upton, Dell, 126n

V notch, 11–13, 36, 38, 41–42; photo of, 38; sketches of, 12
Valley of East Tennessee, 11, 42
Valley of Southwest Virginia, 11, 42
Valley of Virginia, 11
Van Benthuysen, Robert N., Jr., 133n
villages, 15, 47, 49, 56
Vineyard, T.R., 131n
Virginia, 3, 8, 10–11, 13, 16, 42, 44, 85

wagons, 92
Wallace, C., 70
Walland, 97, 124n
walls, 35; construction of, 103, 107
walnut, 60
Warren, M.B., 91; house of, 92
Washington County, Tenn., 70
Waters, James, 78
Weals, Vic, 125n–26n, 131n
wealth, 2, 77, 79, 81, 84, 86, 112; see also affluence
Wear, Samuel, house of, 68
weatherboarding, 69, 85, 106–7, 126n; see also siding
Welsh, 13
Weslager, C.A., 117n–19n
West, 99
West Tennessee, 72
West Virginia, 8, 10, 13
wheat, 72–73, 76, 97
White, Mary, 61, 124n
White County, Ark., 133n
Wildwood, 63, 68, 124n

Wilkerson, Edward, 78
Williams, Andy, xiii
Williams, David, xiii
Williams, Frank B., Jr., 128n
Williams, Michael Ann, 123n
Williamson, Jon, xiii
Willis, Stanley, 3, 118n
Wilms, Douglas, xiii
Wilson, Eugene M., 2, 4, 117n–19n
windows, 24, 103, 105
wood, 31, 35, 42; see also timber
Wood, Beth, xiv
World War I, 3
Worley, Bethany, xiii
Wray, David, xiii–iv
Wynn, Graeme, 125n

yeomen farmers. See farmers

Zelinsky, Wilbur, 3, 87, 118n, 120n, 129n, 133n
Zimolzak, Chester E., 123n

The Log House in East Tennessee
was designed by Betty McDaniel, composed by Lithocraft, Inc.,
and printed and bound by McNaughton & Gunn, Inc.
The book is set in Melior with Gothic Tuscan No. 1 used for display
and printed on 60–lb Glatfelter Natural.